Lady Vols and UConn:
The Greatest Rivalry

Lady Vols and UConn: The Greatest Rivalry

Richard Kent

iUniverse, Inc.
New York Bloomington Shanghai

Lady Vols and UConn: The Greatest Rivalry

Copyright © 2008 by Richard Kent

All rights reserved. No part of this book may be used or reproduced by any means, graphic, electronic, or mechanical, including photocopying, recording, taping or by any information storage retrieval system without the written permission of the publisher except in the case of brief quotations embodied in critical articles and reviews.

iUniverse books may be ordered through booksellers or by contacting:

iUniverse
1663 Liberty Drive
Bloomington, IN 47403
www.iuniverse.com
1-800-Authors (1-800-288-4677)

Because of the dynamic nature of the Internet, any Web addresses or links contained in this book may have changed since publication and may no longer be valid.

The views expressed in this work are solely those of the author and do not necessarily reflect the views of the publisher, and the publisher hereby disclaims any responsibility for them.

ISBN: 978-0-595-48737-0 (pbk)
ISBN: 978-0-595-60827-0 (ebk)

Printed in the United States of America

Contents

Acknowledgments vii
Preface xi
How It All Began 1
The Game That Started It All 3
The Play 9
The Greatest Game 15
The Lowest Common Denominator 21
Past Seasons 24
The Players 47
The Assistants 62
Life After Uconn and Tennessee 72
The Recruiting Wars 84
TASS 92
Is It Still the Greatest Rivalry? 96
Next Seasons 102
Epilogue 111
Top 25 All-Time Largest Home Crowds in Tennessee History 115
College Basketball's Best Rivalries 117
The Greatest Tennessee and Uconn Players by a Vote of Our
    Peers 125

NCAA Champions 127
Uconn and Tennessee Players Who Are Currently Playing in the
    WNBA.. 129
All-Time Results 131
UConn vs. Tennessee Matchups on T.V. Ratings 133

ACKNOWLEDGMENTS

Just so that it is no secret, my favorite women's basketball team is Rutgers, my alma mater even though I am a fan of both Connecticut and the University of Tennessee and I consider UConn-Tennessee to be the top rivalry in the history of women's college basketball.

So why would a 50ish male attorney be interested in writing a book about the Tennessee—Connecticut series? I think that in order to answer that you need to find out why I became interested in women's basketball.

It all stemmed from Rutgers. Despite my alma mater's recent success on the football field and in women's basketball there haven't been a lot of NCAA National Championships running through New Brunswick or Piscataway, New Jersey except in fencing. The women's basketball team did win the AIAW National Championship in Philadelphia in 1982 and my friend, Chris Dailey, the current Associate Women's Head Coach at UConn was a captain of that team and the sixth man. She then moved on to become an assistant coach at Rutgers then to Cornell and then she took a major coaching gamble at the University of Connecticut under a brash former Virginia Assistant Geno Auriemma.

Dailey introduced me to Auriemma in 1985 at a Fairfield-UConn game in Fairfield, Connecticut and Geno and I developed a very cordial relationship. I remain friends with Chris and Geno to this date.

I have asked myself on numerous occasions why I've spent the hundreds of hours necessary to write this book. I certainly love women's college basketball and juxtaposed against men's college basketball and the NBA, feel that it is the only pure basketball left to watch. The NBA is a revolving door of trades and free agency and too many players leave men's college basketball early to play in the pros. Each time I think about the reasons for writing this book I come back to the UConn-Tennessee game in 2001 at the Hartford Civic Center. To say the day before and that day were stormy in Connecticut is an understatement. There were over 20 inches of snow on the ground on the morning of the game and visibility was at an absolute low point. My wife begged me not to make the trip from Westport to

Hartford but I said I had to go and I went and what a game it was. By the way it stopped snowing during the game and the roads were fine on the way back to Westport.

Now why would I have said that I had to go? I guess the reason is either I am crazy or because UConn-Tennessee is a basketball game that simply can't be missed. I certainly hope the latter is the case.

I became enthralled with the women's game as it reminded me a lot of the men's game in the 1960's and specifically the Bill Bradley Princeton teams, who I saw very often playing against Yale at Payne Whitney Gymnasium as I grew up in New Haven, Connecticut. The women's game emphasizes passing, shooting and teamwork as did the men's game in the 1960's and throughout the mid-1970's.

With those events as the background, I started the ten issue Big East Women's Basketball Report with my friend Paul Jaffe about ten years ago. It dealt with all the teams in the Big East and is still going strong ten years later. As a result of that I travel to many women's games both in Hartford and in Piscataway as well as venues throughout the country.

Both places are about an equal distance from my home and on a year in year out basis one will have the opportunity to see all the best teams in the country by just going to Rutgers and Connecticut games. I have continued to do that for the past ten years and have developed some wonderful relationships. As I said I consider Dailey to be a friend, like Auriemma very much and have become an acquaintance of Pat Summitt from Tennessee.

I want to give special thanks to a number of people throughout the college basketball world who have helped me with this specific project. Gail Goestenkors and Tia Jackson then of Duke both spent a tremendous amount of time with me in a hotel lobby up in Hanover, New Hampshire while they were playing in the Dartmouth Invitational in late 2006. Their insights about both Connecticut and Tennessee proved to be invaluable. Randy Press from the UConn Sports Information Department was always available to answer my questions and to fax me information about the series. Summitt was kind enough to return my call at home and we spent a great deal of time on the phone discussing the rivalry. I probably spent even more time with Auriemma during the women's Big East Tournament in Hartford in 2007.

Dailey was always available to answer my questions either by telephone or email and she is one of the most insightful people I have ever run across in the women's college game.

Jen Rizzotti went well beyond the call even having her father watch his tape of the UConn-Tennessee National Championship game in 1995 for me. She is one of the bright minds in women's college basketball and I fully expect her to be the head coach at the University of Connecticut in the future. Holly Warlick, Associate Head Coach at Tennessee helped me out a great deal with her insights as did Shea Ralph, Sue Bird, Diana Taurasi, Tamika Catchings and Michelle Marciniak, all former UConn and Tennessee players. Sue Walvius the head women's coach at South Carolina, Kevin McGuff, the head women's coach at Xavier and Al Brown of Duke were also tremendous resources for me.

I also want to thank Mike DiMauro, Assistant Sports Editor of the New London Day. He is one of the most talented sportswriters in the country and he gave me valuable tips. Special thanks also go to my law partner Michael Meyers, and my friends Howard Ignal and Patt Goldsmith for putting up with my constant chatter about women's basketball and for attending games with me.

This book couldn't have been written without the help of my assistant Lori Schrager and of course the cooperation of my wife, Lisa Kent and my two children who left me alone during my long hours spent at the computer researching and writing this book.

To all of the above people and many more I would like to say "Thanks."

PREFACE

When collegiate women's basketball super power Tennessee and future national rival Connecticut first agreed to meet each other at the midpoint of the 1994-95 season, no one could see at that precise moment that this was a match-up that would propel the sport to an unprecedented level of media coverage.

Fate would have it that by the time the two schools took the court in Connecticut's Gampel Pavilion in the tiny principality of Storrs that winter's day, they had become the last of the unbeatens and held a 1-2 ranking in the polls with Tennessee occupying its traditional position in the top slot.

Because of the nature of its weekly release time, the Associated Press women's poll was put on hold for a 24-hour period to accurately reflect the result of the action from that Monday afternoon.

Appropriately, considering Connecticut coach Geno Auriemma's background growing up in Norristown, Pa., just outside Philadelphia, that afternoon on Martin Luther King Day he and his program were the sport's Rocky Balboa going up against the heavyweights on the other side led by Tennessee's Hall of Fame coach Pat Summitt.

Newspapers from as far away as Los Angeles sent reporters to cover the action.

Connecticut hung tough and produced a stunning upset to earn the Huskies' first-ever No. 1 ranking.

Several months later, the two teams would meet again, this time in Minneapolis for the NCAA championship.

When the Huskies prevailed again, something special had taken hold.

For more than a decade, NCAA titles, No. 1 rankings, or winning streak records were usually at stake as Tennessee-Connecticut became a rivalry by which all others in women's basketball were measured.

It wasn't only the specially skilled players that highlighted the competition. In fact, Connecticut was able to develop superior weaponry through its early successes against the Vols.

But it was also the match-up of personalities between the glib, wise-cracking Auriemma and the no-nonsense, always serious, approach of Summitt that were newsworthy in their own right.

But nothing is forever and suddenly, without warning, just after the arrival of June on the 2007 calendar, it became public that the series was to be no more.

Connecticut announced that Tennessee had not signed the renewed home-and-home contracts, thus creating a stir in an off-season that had taken a while to become calm in the wake of an unprecedented number of coaching changes at major universities.

Of course, there is the excellent potential, considering the talent on both sides, that at least one meeting per year might continue in the NCAA tournament, most likely at the Women's Final Four.

But that possibility aside, fate would also have it that a book has come along just in time to serve as a historical guide to the treasures that were UConn-Tennessee.

It's all there in Lady Vols vs. UConn: The Greatest Rivalry in Women's Basketball by Richard Kent.

This is not hurry-up book timed to take advantage of the news of the rivalry's demise.

Indeed, virtually all the work by the author had been completed by the time the news broke that the series was not going to be renewed.

By day, Richard is a practicing lawyer, who resides in Westport, Conn., with his wife Lisa and two daughters. By night, he is an expert witness not only to the topic he addresses in this book, but also to the sport in general in terms of the number of games he has seen, personally.

Oddly, as a graduate of Rutgers, who also got his law degree at Boston College, Richard could have his emotions affected in the next potential great rivalry now that his alma mater has found a way to beat UConn in Big East competition.

That's an area Richard is quite well versed as the publisher of the Big East women's basketball report during the season.

He's also published Inside Women's College Basketball: Anatomy of a Season and Inside Women's College Basketball: Anatomy of Two Seasons, which are behind-the-scenes examinations of the Huskies' quest for NCAA titles.

In the sports world, Richard has also contributed items to BlackAthlete.Com and SI.Com.

Outside sports, his other works include Fighting for Your Children: A Father's Guide to Custody, and Solomon's Choice.

As for his work on the history of the Tennessee-UConn rivalry, even longtime fans who have watched or attended most, if not all, of the games, will find fascinating insights.

For example, Richard spends time with a chapter discussing the greatest players in the series, who are not necessarily equivalent to the greatest players in the histories of both programs.

Richard notes in the chapter: "Some of the greatest players ever to play in the series either didn't play in enough games to make our list, were injured or didn't have great games in that series but did in their college and pro careers. We hate to leave out the likes of Rebecca Lobo, Kara Wolters, Tamika Catchings, Svetlana Abrosimova, Nykesha Sales and Swin Cash.

On the other hand, "But after careful consideration and analysis along with interviews with coaches and players throughout the country, Shea Ralph, Sue Bird, Chamique Holdsclaw, Semeka Randall and of course the best of them all Diana Taurasi had career game(s) on this the biggest stage in women's college basketball, both regular season and in NCAA games."

In this chapter, Richard also tells the tale of Colleen Healey, who, as a transfer student, began as a team manager, became a walk-on member of the roster, and ultimately received a scholarhip from Auriemma for her spirit and determination.

One chart lists the Top 25 all time crowds in Tennessee history, with the UConn games occupying the top three slots and five of the top 10.

There are breakdowns for the TV ratings of all the games, and also a discussion of the recruiting wars between the two schools.

It was one such skirmish, in fact, not mentioned in the book because of when it was completed, that might have contributed to the untimely end of the series.

Within hours of the news of the cancellation, rumors were centered on Connecticut's successful recruiting over Tennessee of Maya Moore, the top high school prospect in the 2007-08 freshman class, as a major factor in Summitt's decision to cancel the annual showdown.

With all its data, along with the stories, one can envision this book as a handy reference work that could serve as the master arbitrator to resolve heated debates among fans from both schools, especially involving internet message board conversations.

This is certainly a must-have as a matter of historical record as well as a companion piece to the greatest women's basketball rivalry, ever.

Mel Greenberg, a staff writer of The Philadelphia Inquirer who launched the Associated Press women's basketball poll in November, 1976, is a 2007 inductee to the Women's Basketball Hall of Fame in Knoxville, Tenn., for his longtime work in fostering national media coverage of the sport.

He has also been inducted into the Philadelphia Big Five, United States Basketball Writers Association, and Philadelphia Jewish Sports Halls of Fames.

Additionally, Greenberg has received the Big East Media Award, and the College Sports Information Directors Association (CoSIDA) Jake Wade Award that goes to a member of the media for contributions to collegiate athletics.

HOW IT ALL BEGAN

It really all began between UConn and Tennessee after the 1991 Final Four which featured Tennessee, Virginia, Connecticut and Stanford. Tennessee beat Virginia 70-67 in overtime to win the National Championship and Connecticut made its first ever appearance in the Final Four. The Huskies were a heavy underdog in that Final Four, but put themselves on the women's basketball map. Sometime that spring Auriemma approached Summitt on a recruiting trip and broached the idea of playing Tennessee at some point in the future. Summitt was receptive but no deal was put together yet the thought remained in the backs of the minds of both Auriemma and Summitt.

Fast forward to 1993-94. UConn had compiled a 30-3 record losing only at Stanford, at Seton Hall and against North Carolina in the NCAA Tournament in Piscataway, New Jersey. The Huskies were a permanent fixture on the National scene and Tennessee was the premiere Program in the Nation.

Tom Odjakjian, was the college basketball scheduler and guru for ESPN and he was in charge of both men's and women's scheduling at the time. It was a massive task. He had the ability to make or break programs as evidenced by him finally acceding to the requests of Massachusetts men's head coach John Calipari in scheduling the Minutemen for a midnight game to give them some television exposure, at least on the west coast. Odjakjian also did the women's scheduling but it really wasn't much as there were only seven women's games on television that past year, three on CBS and four on ESPN. ESPN covered the Regional finals and CBS covered the two day Final Four.

Odjakjian was getting increasingly busier with the men's scheduling and asked Carol Stiff, a relatively new hire at ESPN in his office and a former coach to schedule the national women's games for 1994-95. There was already in place a Big East-ACC Martin Luther King Day game on ESPN and Stiff looked at the potential teams and knew that she wanted Connecticut from the Big East, if for no other reason than their proximity to Bristol, Connecticut and the fact that they were a burgeoning power. They were returning a great squad and were bringing in High School National Player of the Year Rebecca Lobo from Massachusetts. Odjakjian was very much in favor of playing the game on Martin Luther King Day because there was very little sports competition on other networks and ESPN would most likely be showing a repeat of a tennis match during that time slot. It was also the first year of ESPN2 and there was more available programming for ESPN. Odjakjian had to convince his boss, Loren Matthews but that was an easy sell.

North Carolina of the ACC was going to be quite strong and she contacted head coach Sylvia Hatchell in the spring of 1994 about playing the game on television on the afternoon of Martin Luther King Day in January. Hatchell wanted to play the game but she wanted to play it at her place. Stiff told her that the game had to be at the Big East venue and Hatchell surprisingly demurred. A few other ACC teams were contacted and nothing developed.

Stiff then got in touch with UConn Associate Athletic Director Jeff Hathaway. Hathaway is now the UConn Athletic Director. Hathaway talked to Auriemma and Auriemma very much wanted him to contact Tennessee of the SEC. Stiff had no problem with that and he contacted women's athletic director Joan Cronan with whom he had a relationship from his days as an assistant athletic director at Maryland. Cronan talked to Summitt and Summitt was somewhat reluctant to play the game because she already had her SEC schedule in front of her and knew that there were a number of games bunched around Martin Luther King Day and it would be difficult to make a trip up to Connecticut.

If you know anything about Summitt, you know that she was all about marketing and promoting women's college basketball on the national scene as well as winning. She does all of them better than any coach in the country. She thought about it for a few minutes and said "it is for the good of the game so I will play it." Thus the game was set for January 16, 1995 in Storrs. The Hartford Civic Center was never a consideration because the UConn women had never played a game there yet and didn't even sell out Gampel for all of their games. Also and coincidentally UConn was playing Georgetown at the Hartford Civic Center on the night of Martin Luther King Day in 1995 so the January, 1995 game was a unique "doubleheader" for UConn and somewhat of a taxing logistical issue for their Sports Information Department. The rest is history and continues to make history in the women's game.

THE GAME THAT STARTED IT ALL

It is impossible to quantify whether or not it was the greatest women's college basketball game ever played and in reality we have chosen the 2000 game at Gampel as the most exciting, but in all likelihood the 1995 National Championship game was the most important not only for the rivalry but for women's college basketball as a whole.

The 1995 National Championship game between UConn and Tennessee in Minneapolis, for lack of a better term, raised awareness for the game as no game had before. No matter all the game's great stories to that date, from Texas' 34-0 season to Stanford's two titles, to Tennessee's multiple national championships, to the greatness at Old Dominion and Louisiana Tech—not even back to the great Cathy Rush at Immaculata—had ever generated the attention for the game than an early April Sunday in 1995.

People in Tennessee, and perhaps other parts of the country where the women's game flourished, might have bristled that the Jenny-come-latelys at UConn didn't merely become the game's darlings, but became what felt like the game's face. How could that be possible for a team that had never won a national championship and had been to only one Final Four?

Easy. The answer is proximity.

Connecticut's location, between media hubs Boston and New York, as well as being home to ESPN, gives UConn a quicker path to the most attention than any other team in the country. The New York Times and Boston Globe didn't merely send reporters to Minneapolis to watch UConn-Tennessee, but suddenly found a local interest. And when the Times has a local interest, the story goes national.

Suddenly, all the stories than had intoxicated Connecticut became stories for the nation. Suddenly, Rebecca Lobo's puckish sense of humor—she once said Julia Child is one of three people in history she'd invite to dinner because someone had to cook—became national charm. Jennifer Rizzotti's linebacker mentality at 5-foot-5 and her rivalry with Michelle Marciniak gave sports fans two appetizing storylines: the little kid who could mixed with a personal rivalry against another great player.

Then there was Geno Auriemma. The game never had a personality like this. He made the media's job more fun. He made the media want to go to the games because of what he might say next. It was no knock against Pat Summitt, who had always been gracious and accommodating. But Auriemma's wise guy Philadelphia mien was just too delicious to resist.

And so came the day of the game. UConn, at 34-0, brought so many subplots to the championship game. In a way, the Huskies were underdogs, even though they hadn't lost. They were the darling upstarts playing the Internal Revenue Service. Auriemma would late call Tennessee the "Microsoft" of women's basketball.

The game even made for a better story. UConn had to rally from a nine-point deficit at halftime, not to mention some serious foul trouble to Rizzotti, Lobo and Nykesha Sales, UConn's three All-Americans.

The foul trouble forced UConn into its second halftime deficit that season, 38-32. Lobo, Rizzotti and Sales each had three fouls and Wolters two. A year later, Auriemma yelled across the floor to UConn beat writers during a UConn-Tennessee game in Knoxville, "now you see why they've won 69 in a row," alluding to the Lady Vols' 69-game home court win streak and what he believed was questionable officiating. The seeds of the away games are officiated with Tennessee were planted in this game.

The Lady Vols led by as many as six points four times and had the six-point lead at the half when Laurie Milligan ended it with a jumper.

"At halftime, I said we can't possibly do anything worse than we did the first 20 minutes, and we were only down six," Auriemma told reporters after the game. "I felt good—and fortunate.... It was a simple halftime talk. I told the team that if we outrebounded them in the second half, we'll win the game."

Summitt said, "We missed the front end of three one-and-ones, so it should have been a 10- or 12-point lead at halftime. But the first half didn't cost us the game. We're a second-half team, but a big factor was that at the first dead-ball timeout of the second half, UConn had a 12-3 rebounding lead. That forced us to struggle in transition."

Despite that, Tennessee had a nine-point lead with 18 minutes left on a Latina Davis jump shot. The Huskies cut it to one three minutes later. And then Lobo, who was whistled for her third foul only 7:10 into the game, managed to stay on the floor long enough in the second half to hit four of her first five shots to give UConn a 58-55 led with eight minutes left.

Later in the second half with UConn clinging to a lead, Rizzotti authored, to that point, the second-most memorable play in the history of the game, probably behind Charlotte Smith's 3-point field goal that won North Carolina a national championship.

Rizzotti's crossover dribble spun Marciniak, who was nicknamed "Spinderella." Rizzotti zipped to the basket and scored, giving UConn fans the play of a lifetime.

Lobo, who had 17 points, was named Final Four MVP.

Auriemma, meanwhile, was carried off the floor, just after Lobo took a victory lap around the Target Center. Auriemma took a call from President Clinton a few minutes later.

Auriemma said after UConn beat Stanford that the Huskies "couldn't stumble into history," but said after this game that fate was there for them.

"It would be really hard for me to express how I feel to play that game the way it was played and beat a team that's as good as any I've seen in college basketball," Auriemma said. "To win that game is the greatest feeling I've ever had, and I'm delighted my players were given the opportunity to show the talents they have."

The next 24 hours were, arguably, the most special in the history of the program. A celebration went long in to the night. Meghan Culmo, who has become a color analyst during UConn broadcasts and was part of the program's first Final Four team in 1991, remembered leaving the party so late that the USA Today was just being delivered to the hotel rooms.

Someone decided to begin watching the game tape late into the night. When Auriemma began to critique their play, as he usually did, Missy Rose, a reserve guard, playfully flashed her middle finger at her coach and said, "too late now, baby."

Rose, when reminded of those years after she graduated, blushed. She is the assistant principal at a Pennsylvania school.

Columnist Owen Canfield of the Hartford Courant, anticipating the team's flight home on Monday, wrote, "The NCAA Division I women's college basketball championship flag will fly over the state university in Storrs. They should haul it down and have it dry-cleaned every day just to preserve the purity of the memorable season that ended with a surging, 70-64 victory over Tennessee at the Target Center. The Huskies wound up 35-0. That's pure. Hey, Connecticut, let's have a parade. Bet you already have started planning back there? Wait for us, we who traveled here to watch. We'll be home today."

Unbelievable couldn't begin to describe what awaited UConn. The team plane landed about 6 p.m. What the players and coaches didn't know was the thousands and thousands of people waiting for them.

It began at Bradley International Airport, where thousands of fans waited several hours in chilly spring weather.

Five to six deep, fans peered though the chain link fence cheering, shouting and waving banners, signs and pompoms. Windsor Locks firefighters even showed a congratulatory sign on one of the ladders.

On the way to campus, banners were everywhere. On overpasses from the I-291 ramp in East Hartford to Exit 68 in Tolland. The state Department of Transportation had illuminated the electronic road signs on the highway with, "UConn Women's Basketball, National Champions 1995."

But it was back at campus where 8,000 fans, nearly filling Gampel Pavilion for all of Monday afternoon into night, that turned it into an event.

When the team entered Gampel to everyone singing, "We Are The Champions," the jaws of the players and coaches hit the floor in disbelief—that this many people would show up. Pam Webber looked around in complete wonder, mouthing the words, "Oh my God" over and over. It was Camelot.

"I'm really shaking. I can't find words for what this means to me," Webber said, nearly crying tears of joy. "I feel so blessed to have had my life touched by so many wonderful people. That goes for my best friends, my coaches and you people here."

Lobo told the crowd, "We think we have something special here … and, in a way, it has nothing to do with the basketball court, but it has to do with how we feel about each other and you."

Lobo didn't spend much time on campus. She appeared on "Late Night With David Letterman," a night later. Lobo went with Auriemma, associate head coach Chris Dailey, associate director of athletic communications Barb Kowal and teammate Jamelle Elliot.

The repartee was priceless.

Letterman: "Your coach is a man, isn't he? What is that like? Is that legal? Shouldn't they have a female coach? … The women of the team don't mind having a male coach?"

Lobo: "No, not at all. And he's not bad looking either, so we don't mind."

Letterman asked Lobo about a professional career. There was no WNBA at the time.

"You can make decent money, not like the men make, but you can make all right money over there," Lobo said.

And then Lobo talked about aspirations to be a sports broadcaster. Lobo, who married a sportswriter (Steve Rushin, formerly of Sports Illustrated) fulfilled her dream. She's a lead analyst and sideline reporter for ESPN.

The UConn women's program exploded after that. Gampel Pavilion and later the Hartford Civic Center became sold out for every game. Tickets were being scalped—for hundreds of dollars when Tennessee was in town. Every game was televised either on ESPN, CBS or Connecticut Public Television. The UConn Athletic Department has made millions of dollars on the women's program at UConn. The rumor is that only three women's programs nationally make money for the universities and UConn and Tennessee are two of them.

Never in Connecticut and never across the country had or has a team engendered so many new fans as a result of one game regardless of gender, age or educational background. And the beat goes on a full 12 years later.

THE PLAY

The play that helped to define UConn women's basketball and the UConn-Tennessee series more than any single act or play in the history of the long and storied series took place in 1995 in Minneapolis towards the end of the National Championship game.

First the players, the protagonists. Michelle Marciniak was the National High School Player of the Year a year before Rizzotti and in the same class as Lobo. Rizzotti was a very good high school player in Connecticut but was not highly recruited. Her final choices game down to Providence, Rutgers and Connecticut. She chose Connecticut because she bought into Coach Auriemma's vision as well as the chance to play with a dominant center in Lobo.

In baseball parlance, Thompson and Branca are linked at the hip. In men's basketball it is Magic and Bird. In golf you can't say Palmer without saying Nicklaus.

In discussing UConn-Tennessee rivalry the names Michelle Marciniak and Jen Rizzotti are also inextricably woven together, probably more as a function of one particular play in the 1996 Championship game in Minneapolis than anything else.

Rizzotti is now the head coach at the University of Hartford and has not unexpectedly built the women's basketball program into an America East power in just seven years, winning three Conference championships over the past three years and making three trips to the NCAA tournament. The University is located in West Hartford in a tranquil setting. Pre-Rizzotti the most recognizable face on campus was Vin Baker who later played in the NBA with the Bucks and the Sonics. Even Baker's teams at Hartford didn't come close to winning the league championship under men's head coach Paul Brazeau.

Marciniak is now an assistant basketball coach at the University of South Carolina with much of her duties relating to recruiting. She is still an avid Tennessee fan.

There were approximately a minute and fifty three seconds remaining in the 1995 National Championship game in Minneapolis. UConn was playing Tennessee. UConn had never been there before. Tennessee had been there and won many times. Tennessee had led most of the way despite having lost to UConn earlier in the season at Gampel and the game was tied at 61. Tennessee had just called a time out and had set up a play for future WNBA star Nikki McCray. After the ball was inbounded McCray took about a twenty footer and it bounced off the rim and the long rebound ended in the hands of Jennifer Rizzotti, UConn's star point guard. Rizzotti looked down the court and saw only a one on three opportunity for herself but was able to weave through two defenders and the only Tennessee player between her and the basket and a UConn lead was Michelle Marciniak. Marciniak went for the strip and in the process Rizzotti switched hands from her right hand to her equally adept left hand, passed Marciniak and went in unmolested for a lefty lay up. The rest was history. UConn would win its first National Championship 70-64 in Minneapolis and Rizzotti would find herself on the cover of Sports Illustrated with that nifty lefty move.

UConn was in trouble through most of the first half as Rizzotti and Lobo had three fouls apiece and Wolters had two. Rizzotti had four points and no assists at the half, certainly not a Jen Rizzotti half of basketball.

At times as a Husky, Rizzotti even sounded like a coach. She was always the star of the media room after games, answering questions not like a twenty year old college junior but like a future coach, questioning reporters on all aspects and angles of their questions.

Most recently she led the Hawks to the Program's first ever victory in the NCAA tournament over 19th ranked Temple. The win over Temple was the first in school history against a nationally ranked opponent. Hartford finished the season of 2005-06 with a 27-4 record, setting a school record for overall wins in conference victories at 15. Rizzotti was named America East Coach of the Year. Rizzotti is the winningest coach in school history.

During a great deal of her early coaching career at Hartford Rizzotti played for the three time WNBA Champion Houston Comets and their Hall of Fame head coach and current LSU head coach Van Chancelor. She learned a lot from Chancelor as she had from Auriemma at UConn.

If a war was going on and I could have been in a bunker with anyone I would have to chose Jen. She is just so heady, take charge and confident that I know she would get me out of it. So said an 8 month pregnant Kara Wolters in discussing Rizzotti, her former teammate. The play changed the momentum of the game completely. We thought we could win before it and knew we would win after it because we finally had the lead in the second half despite being in deep foul trouble. Jen never talks about the play. It was just another day at work for her. I wanted to hate Marciniak both before and after that game because she went to Tennessee but she was my roommate later on one summer for purposes of USA Basketball and I really like her, but it was only Jen who could have made that play. Keesha was a freshman and still too young and Rebecca, JJ and myself would never have had the ability to dribble down court in between defenders like she did.

Rizzotti calls it the "signature play of (my) career." She says this largely because of the impact that it had on the media and her appearance on the cover of Sports Illustrated. Rizzotti is a very humble individual and she ignores to say that it was probably the pivotal play in UConn's first national championship game. She even goes as far as to say that Lobo was the poster child for that team and she was surprised that Lobo was not on the cover of Sports Illustrated. She feels that the only reason that she was on the cover was because a Sports Illustrated photographer had a great angle on the shot. Her self-deprecating style is a welcome one in an era where athletes have huge egos.

The paths taken by both Rizzotti and Marciniak to that ultimate showdown at the free throw line in Minneapolis are as varied as any two players on any basketball teams.

Marciniak as previously mentioned was the 1991 National High School Player of the Year as a senior at Allentown Central Catholic High School in Allentown, Pennsylvania. She scored 3,025 points for Central Catholic and her no. 23 jersey has since been retired by the school.

Marciniak was recruited heavily by every major program in the country and narrowed her choices down to Notre Dame, Tennessee, Texas and Stanford. She ultimately chose Notre Dame despite getting a scholarship offer from Tennessee. She chose Notre Dame largely because of her Catholic upbringing and the fact that after she got her offer from Tennessee and before the advent of cell phones Tennessee got a verbal commitment from a star guard from Tennessee. Marciniak would have had the chance to also attend Tennessee but chose to go another route. After a year she left the University of Notre Dame largely because they lost seventeen games and enrolled at the University of Tennessee with the blessings of Summitt.

With Marciniak at point guard, the Lady Vols won consecutive Southern Conference championships in 1995 and 96 and won it all in 1996. Marciniak was chosen as the Final Four's Most Valuable Player that year.

After three seasons in the American Basketball League, Marciniak was signed by the WNBA expansion team Portland Fire in 2000 and played for one season. In 2002 she retired from basketball to become an assistant coach at the University of South Carolina. She is also an occasional color analyst for WNBA and NCAA basketball games.

Bob Picozzi was the sports anchor for WTNH Channel 8 in New Haven at the time of the game and was at press row. He noted that there was a discernable momentum switch once the play happened. That play made him and many members of the press think that UConn could win. He focused on the play in his 6:00 p.m. newscast from outside of the arena and led with highlights of it at 11:00 p.m. that night.

Marciniak models much of what she does on a daily basis after Summitt. She tries to emulate her coaching style and freely says that "Pat made me the person that I am today." It is Summitt's intensity that really draws Marciniak to her even as a rival coach in the SEC.

When Marciniak entered the University of Tennessee the school's big rivals were Georgia, Vanderbilt, Louisiana Tech, Old Dominion and Stanford. UConn wasn't even on the radar screen and even though Auriemma recruited her she did not even pay them a visit despite her location in Pennsylvania.

When Connecticut emerged in 1995 as a major player on the national scene Marciniak was stunned. She remembered them as a middling team in the Big East and watched in some disbelief as her team fell to UConn during the 1994 regular season in Storrs.

Jen-Michelle was the key match-up of the game. Jen was huge to our team, on the court and off the court. I was trailing the play but got a good look at it. Jen made a great move to the basket and scored. That really got our bench into it and made us feel that we could and would win the game. Jamelle Elliot is now an assistant coach at UConn and will never forget the magic in Minnesota.

It was really the National Championship game in Minneapolis in 1995 that forever linked Marciniak and Rizzotti. When asked about that game and the play at the end of the game Marciniak's response was "you really had to ask me about that." She was of course kidding but she recognizes that Rizzotti's drive by her towards the end of the game to give UConn the lead and ultimately a 70-64 victory for the national championship was one of the most remembered plays in the history of women's college basketball and landed Rizzotti on the cover of Sports Illustrated. She bemoans the fact that she did not tie her up or foul her.

Marciniak played against Rizzotti in the ABL and both of them were "competitors first." She did add that she and Rizzotti are now friendly and the rivalry has grown more into "mutual respect" over the years.

Marciniak and Rizzotti often see each other on the recruiting trails or at the Final Four. They rarely if ever talk about the play and instead exchange pleasantries about their careers and families. The play speaks for itself. It defined Rizzotti's career and to some extent Marciniak's playing career. Marciniak on occasion has questioned whether or not she should have committed a foul as soon as Rizzotti switched hands and it was clear that she could not strip the ball. It might have taken some emotion out of the ultimate score but that is a lot of thinking to go on in the head of an athlete in a split second of time.

Last year Rizzotti's Hartford team played at South Carolina in the WNIT. South Carolina won easily and Rizzotti and Marciniak never exchanged any words about the play. There is no doubt though that it was still in the back of both of their minds when they saw each other at mid court to exchange handshakes both before and after the game.

Rizzotti is a very humble individual and she ignores responding when it is mentioned to her that it was probably the pivotal play in UConn's first National Championship game. She even goes so far as to say that Rebecca Lobo was the poster child for that team and she was surprised that Lobo, instead of her was not on the cover of that Sports Illustrated. She feels that the only reason that she was on the cover was because a Sports Illustrated photographer had a great angle on the play. Her self-deprecating style is a welcome one in an era where athletes have huge egos.

You know it was a lucky bounce. Jen was not exactly the best rebounder in the world but she did have a knack for being in the right place at the right time. If someone else had gotten the ball they never would have made the play that she did. But I must say that I never doubted that we were going to win that day. If it hadn't been that play Jen or someone else would have made a big play later on in the day. Auriemma is not a big one for compliments but he knew even after saying those words that it was more than a lucky bounce.

The play is something that Rizzotti still deals with if not on a daily basis. She figures that she signs about six Sports Illustrated covers a year and constantly gets teased by her ever changing players on the University of Hartford team for her hairstyle as depicted on that Sports Illustrated cover.

Rizzotti was one if not the most popular player in the history of University of Connecticut women's basketball and was recently elected into the UConn Wall of Fame. It is that one play though that seems to stick in the minds of fans at UConn games more than any other during her illustrious four year career in Storrs.

Lobo thought long and hard about the significance of the play and noted that "who knows what would have happened to women's hoops at UConn and in general if we hadn't won the game thanks to the efforts of Jen. I'm glad we didn't find out." Well spoken Rebecca.

Summitt said that the play "put a stamp on the win." It still stands out in her mind. She notes that "I have watched the tape of that game many times and it is the signature play." Summitt has said on many occasions that "big players come up big" and that was certainly epitomized by Rizzotti's heroics."

Nancy Lieberman, a commentator for ESPN and one of the greatest women's players of all time noted that Rizzotti's play, "put UConn on the basketball map." She was not surprised by anything about the play as it epitomized Rizzotti's style as a hard-nosed blue collar worker. Not a whole lot unlike Lieberman's game when she was a star for Old Dominion and in the pros.

Many feel that Rizzotti is the heir apparent to Auriemma at UConn. Marciniak should also end up as a head coach at a major program, probably in the SEC.

THE GREATEST GAME

Tennessee entered basketball year 1999-2000 with plenty of unanswered questions and the start of what many would construe to be a new era.

The best player in the history of Tennessee women's basketball, Chamique Holdsclaw had graduated.

Tennessee certainly had one of the best players in the country in Tamika Catchings, an All-American. But despite the presence of Catchings and a talented group of juniors Tennessee was not ranked no. 1 in any of the preseason polls. That was in direct contrast to the prior three years when Tennessee was virtually everyones' number 1 preseason.

Tennessee did return its emotional leader in Semeka Randall from Cleveland and star point guard Kristen "Ace" Clement from Philadelphia. Tennessee had made a concerted decision to recruit Clement and not UConn's star point guard Sue Bird from New York City. Going into their junior seasons many scribes questioned the wisdom of that decision.

Tennessee was bringing in freshman Kara Lawson and April McDivitt along with 6'2" forward Gwen Jackson.

The Lady Vols went to Europe in August and ran up a 5-0 record against some healthy competition.

They beat the U.S. National Team on November 7, no small feat but a week later lost their home opener to Louisiana Tech 69-64. They were highly favored in the game and in the process lost their 40 game home winning streak and their 17 straight opening game victories.

It was clear after this game that Clement was struggling at the point and seemed to lack both the confidence and the leadership to lead the team.

The Lady Vols entered their January 8, 2000 home contest against UConn without a great deal of confidence. The team wasn't clicking on all cylinders from a defensive perspective and Clement was still struggling at the point guard position. Summitt considered moving Lawson to the point but felt that it was still too early in her tenure to make such a dramatic move, especially with a game against a foe as talented as UConn.

Tennessee was coming off of three straight wins against UConn and had not lost two games at home since losing to Stanford and Georgia during the 1996-97 season.

Summitt's team led 25-24 in the first half but trailed 43-37 at half time and never again took the lead. They shot only 28.6 percent from the field in the second half and fell 74-67. Tennessee started to make a move and with 2:57 left UConn held only a 3 point lead. Tennessee center Michelle Snow was then fouled by UConn center Paige Sauer and after the foul Snow spiked the ball on the court and received a controversial technical foul. Snow missed both of her free throws and Bird went to the foul line for the technical, made the second shot and the rest was history. Randall led Tennessee with 20 points and Bird scored a career high 25. Shea Ralph had an all around great game with 13 points, 8 rebounds and 5 assists.

After the game the UConn players danced around at center court and pointed to their fans in the stands. Both Summitt and her team remembered that incident a scant 25 days later when they traveled to Gampel to resume their bitter rivalry.

About two weeks before the Gampel game Georgia embarrassed Tennessee on national television 78-51 on Martin Luther King Day this was the Lady Vols worse SEC lost ever.

Summitt made a big decision after that loss and moved Clement to shooting guard and put Lawson, the freshman in as a starter at the point backed up by another freshman McDivett. It was really point guard by committee at that point in time.

The two teams met again on February 2, 2000 and UConn entered the game with a 19 game winning streak and an undefeated ledger.

Most predicted that UConn would handle Tennessee easily at home despite only beating Boston College by 7 points about a week earlier on the road. The first half did not disappoint the sold out UConn faithful. UConn jumped out to a 5-0 lead and led 29-15 towards the end of the first half. The lead stayed constant at 34-20 and the Huskies were up by 11 with 1:41 remaining in the half. In the final 34 seconds of the half Randall made a lay up and Catchings hit a three pointer and UConn only led by 6 points.

Two minutes into the second half Tennessee had taken a 1 point lead and with 7:17 left to play led by 9.

UConn then took over in this seesaw battle with a run of its own fueled by Tamika Williams and with 3:45 to play the game was tied at 65. During a time out Randall made it clear to her teammates that it was her turn to take over the game. She was not only the emotional leader of the team but the leader on the court. Randall banked in a shot with 27 seconds to play to give Tennessee a 1 point lead and then Bird answered with her own field goal to give the Huskies the lead. Randall then demanded the ball and willed in a 12 foot shot with Bird's hand in her face with 4.4 seconds to play.

UConn called two times out to map out strategy for a play but missed at the buzzer and Tennessee had the upset.

There had been other great games in the history of the UConn-Tennessee and we will chronicle some of them.

One can't ignore the first game ever played between the two teams on January 16, 1995 at Gampel in which the Lady Vols were number one in the country and the Huskies were number 2. Connecticut was the new kid on the block and Tennessee was the established power with five national championships. UConn won the game 77-66 to put themselves on the basketball map.

As mentioned in another chapter in this book the epic national championship game of April 2, 1995 in which UConn won 70-64 at Minneapolis to win it's first national championship and to become the second team in NCAA history to post an undefeated season was huge for the game of women's basketball.

How can anyone forget March 29, 1996 in a battle of number one seeds in which the Vols eliminated UConn in the national semi-finals in overtime to win the first of three straight NCAA titles behind Chamique Holdsclaw.

No one will ever forget the January 4, 2003 game in which UConn beat Tennessee 63-62 in overtime. Diana Taurasi was the star of that game with a 25 point performance that included a tying shot in regulation with 7.5 seconds left and the game winner with 31 seconds left in overtime. What can't be forgotten is that Taurasi made a 3 pointer from about 60 feet away as time expired in the first half to put UConn ahead 29-26.

The game that we chose though was held on February 2, 2000, once again at Gampel. UConn was arguably the greatest team to ever play the game of women's college basketball and that fact was validated on two other occasions during that season. At a time in which UConn and Tennessee played twice during the year Connecticut had defeated Tennessee 74-67 at Tennessee in January behind Sue Bird's 25 points and won the National Championship 71-52 in Philadelphia in April behind Shea Ralph's 15 points on 7-8 shooting from the field.

What many people forget is that on February 2 of that year the number 1 Huskies fell to the number 4 Lady Vols 72-71 at home on the strength of a 15 foot Semeka Randall runner with 4.4 seconds left, for the Huskies' only loss of the season.

The media attention for that game was perhaps larger than any regular season game between UConn and Tennessee. The reason for that is not fully known but the build up in both Connecticut and Tennessee was beyond belief. Al Brown, who is an Assistant Coach at Tennessee and is currently an assistant women's coach at Duke said that "the intensity of that game for forty minutes was probably stronger than any UConn Tennessee game I had witnessed in my tenure as an assistant coach under Pat." During the first half of that game Randall in going for a loose ball actually ended up on the scorer's table at half court.

The Lady Vols were down 6 points at the half and it seemed like at least 10 to most in the sold out and highly partisan UConn crowd. Both Coach Summitt and junior Kyra Elzy gave scintillating half time speeches and the Lady Vols, then 16-3 rallied with a dozen points off second chances in the second half to beat UConn.

The Huskies held Randall, the emotional leader of the team to 4 points in the first half but Randall had 13 in the second half and 6 in the final two minutes of the game. Tamika Catchings was a monster off of the boards with 13 rebounds and noted after the game that "I saw the look in (Randall's) eyes and knew that she was going to take over the game in the second half."

The Huskies had one more chance to win after the Randall score. Svetlana Abrosimova took the inbounds pass and got the ball to Tamika Williams. Williams was guarded by freshman Michelle Snow and her shot bounced off the bottom of the rim in the last second.

Coach Auriemma was not happy at all with his teams effort and said after the game, "every time we made a mistake they made us pay for it. We reacted like a young team."

The Lady Vols trailed by as many as 13 points in the first half but then went on a 15-0 run towards the end of the first half and into the second half to give Tennessee it's first lead at 36-34—no one went on a 15-0 run against UConn, especially at Gampel.

Shea Ralph remembers the game quite well. She agrees that it was one of the most intense games she had ever been involved in. UConn had won narrowly on the road and Tennessee wanted revenge. It was the first game between the two foes ever played at Gampel and that added a lot of incentive for UConn because the crowd is closer to the court and much louder. UConn also hired the famous "let's get ready to rumble" announcer and that really juiced up not only the crowd but the players but in retrospect also the Tennessee players. Ralph guarded Randall during that game and said that she was "such a competitor it was tough to stop her." And for Ralph to say that it was tough to stop somebody defensively says a whole heckofa lot about their play.

She further noted that the game was definitely incentive for UConn going into the National Championship game in Philadelphia later that year because it was their only loss of the season. Auriemma usually gets upset about the loss but he and the coaching staff treated the game very philosophically after it ended. It might have been a relief for him to finally have one loss on the ledger and not have to face a national championship game undefeated. He also recognized and told his team that they had a lot of fight during the game and unlike the Iowa State game in the Sweet Sixteen in 1999 never folded.

Niya Butts played for Tennessee at the time as a fifth year senior. She said that her team was very disappointed about the loss in Knoxville in January because they felt as a whole that Tennessee had equivalent talent but that UConn was getting all the publicity. That gave the Lady Vols a great deal of incentive heading into Storrs in February. She said that there was "a lot of pride on the line in that game for sure." She also noted that it is even tougher to win at Gampel than at the Hartford Civic Center so there was an added component of difficulty right from the get go. She remembered that after Randall's shot went in her team jumped up and ran around like "crazy people." She concluded by saying that Tennessee had "bragging rights" right until the National Championship game in Philadelphia.

Randall remembers the game very vividly. She had a tussle with Abrosimova towards the end of the first half and every time she touched the ball in the second half she heard the boobirds. She had never experienced anything like that in her high school or college career.

She further added that the play at the end of the game was not meant for her but actually meant for Tamika Catchings who is known as a better outside shooter but Randall got herself open and took the shot. She noted that it was the only game winning shot of her career and it is a game that she will never forget.

Summitt agrees that the game at Gampel was indeed the greatest regular season game between UConn and Tennessee in their storied history. It was the only game decided on a last second shot and she characterized the environment in Connecticut at the time as being "great." She felt fortunate to win but would have rather have won the National Championship in Philadelphia later that year.

THE LOWEST COMMON DENOMINATOR

Harry Perretta is the head women's basketball coach at Villanova University in Pennsylvania. He has held that position for 27 years and has established himself as one of the most respected and knowledgeable coaches in the country, especially as it relates to his motion offense.

He has tallied a career record of 507-282 making him the 21st winningest active collegiate coach and the all-time winningest coach in the history of Villanova basketball for both men and women.

The 2002-03 season was probably the most special one for Perretta as he led his team to a 28-6 overall record and a 12-4 record in the Big East and to an improbable 52-48 upset over Connecticut in New Jersey to win the Big East Tournament. The Wildcats advanced to the Elite Eight for the first and only time in school history that year, losing to Tennessee at Knoxville. More later about Tennessee.

Perretta has known Auriemma for over 30 years. They are both from Philadelphia and when Auriemma was an assistant women's basketball coach at St. Joseph's under Jim Foster, Perretta was a young head coach at Villanova. They immediately hit it off and spent many long lunches together talking basketball. They thought alike and had similar defensive philosophies. Both had played basketball in Catholic leagues and Philadelphia. During that time frame the St. Joseph's team beat Villanova more often than not but the series was close. It certainly didn't hinder the relationship between Peretta and Auriemma.

Fast forward to the spring of 2002 at Boo Williams Basketball Camp in Virginia. Boo Williams is one if not the premier recruiting camp in the country for high school women's basketball players and all major Division I coaches attend it on a yearly basis. That year Perretta was walking by the stands and saw his friend Cathy Inglese, head coach at Boston College. He went up to talk to her and

Inglese happened to be sitting next to Summitt. Perretta had never met Summitt and Inglese introduced him to her. They hit it off and at some point during the conversation Summitt asked Perretta if she could pick his brain about the highly successful motion offense that he ran. He gave her his cell number and never really expected to hear from her. A few weeks later she called him and asked if she could fly up to Philadelphia with her staff to sit and listen through a Perretta tutelage about the motion offense in his gym. He said fine and actually called Auriemma joking about it. Auriemma thought it was great and wished him luck.

Perretta met with Summitt and her assistants in Pennsylvania for a few hours and went over the offense and shared knowledge with her about her offense at Tennessee.

When the public heard about Perretta and Summitt through newspaper accounts of the meeting certain writers and fans made a lot more about it than it was probably worth. Auriemma then stepped in as he is want to do and cracked a number of jokes about what he characterized as the "relationship" and there was even an article in the New York Times about the new fast coaching friends, Pat and Harry. Ironically that next year and as previously mentioned Perretta's team made it to the Elite Eight in Knoxville. They faced Tennessee and lost to them as Tennessee went to the Final Four. The night before the game Perretta and his team were invited over to Summitt's spacious house with a few reporters. Summitt has a hot tub at her house and Geno then made a number of jokes about Perretta and Summitt in the hot tub, none of which were true and it was all in good humor.

Perretta is a huge fan of both Geno and Pat and feel that they are the top coaches in the game. He also feels that they have a lot of coaching similarities. Both of their programs have very proud traditions but he said what separates them from other coaches is that they work really hard at getting very talented players and succeed in getting the best players in the country. He mused about what it would be like for Villanova with more talented players to run his motion offense but quickly dismissed that thought knowing that he is most likely never going to get the elite players like Geno and Pat. He feels that both UConn and Tennessee are very disciplined oriented both on and off the court and both run multiple defenses and on occasion triangles on offense. He observed that Tennessee pushes the ball down court more but when UConn had the Bird, Cash and Taurasi teams in the early 2000's they did the same thing. Peretta looks for UConn to run a similar offense this coming year.

Perretta feels that the rivalry between UConn and Tennessee is as big as it ever was and will continue getting bigger as long as Pat and Geno are on their respective campuses. He thinks that it is really good for the rivalry that Tennessee has won the last two games and finally won another National Championship this past year, breaking a nine year drought.

Perretta is a very loyal guy and while he likes both Geno and Pat he always roots for the Big East team and thus UConn when the two teams meet in a regular season or NCAA game. He even rooted for Rutgers this past year in Cleveland against Tennessee and told Summitt that. Pat had no problem with that as she is likewise loyal to the SEC teams.

Perretta feels that both UConn and Tennessee will vie for the National Championship this coming season and in reality when each season starts, no matter what the talent level is at either or both schools he feels that both teams have about an equal shot of making it to the Final Four. He admires both Programs that much.

PAST SEASONS

The University of Connecticut women's basketball team made it to the Elite Eight in 2005-06 at Harbor Yards in Bridgeport, Connecticut before losing in overtime to Duke.

Few can doubt that they overachieved that year and in the process lost three key components to their team by way of graduation namely, Barbara Turner, Ann Strother and Wilnett Crockett. Turner was the guts of the team and hit the key three at the buzzer to surprisingly send the Duke game into overtime. She also was easily the team's hustle winner and despite her short stature led the team in rebounding on many occasions. Strother hit many timely shots.

The Huskies entered 2006-07 with a proven commodity in speedy sophomore guard Renee Montgomery, a sharp shooting but sometimes slow afoot Mel Thomas who was injured a great deal the season before after suffering an ankle injury at Syracuse, quick Ketia Swanier who shared some time with Montgomery at the point, inconsistent junior forward Charde Houston and often injured Duke transfer center Brittany Hunter. The Huskies brought in a talented freshman in Tina Charles, the consensus national high school player of the year during her senior season as Christ the King in Jamaica, New York. She was also the 2006 McDonalds and Gatorade National Player of the Year. She attended the same high school as former Husky Sue Bird.

Most preseason magazines had UConn tabbed anywhere between seven and ten nationally. Many thought that might be a tad high. The three graduating seniors were proven players and leaders and the best returning player, Houston was so inconsistent as a sophomore that she didn't even score in the key Duke game. Her enigmatic play was puzzling to Auriemma and there was a great deal of talk during the off season that she would transfer. Auriemma joked that it wasn't until she returned for the team picture in September that he knew that she was back on the squad.

Depth, especially at the post and forward positions was considered to be a real issue during the season.

After October the Big East women's basketball coaches tabbed UConn as no. 1 in Conference pre-season but only slightly ahead of Rutgers who went into the season with a three game winning streak against UConn. It was also felt by the coaches that DePaul, Louisville and Pittsburgh were going to be very strong so it was clear at least in October that UConn had a lot of work in front of it to achieve as much as it did in the previous season, Auriemma's 21st at UConn.

Auriemma indicated during the Big East meetings at the ESPN Zone in New York that he felt that if the pieces fell in place he had a Final Four team this year. Few on the National scene at that point in time would have agreed with him especially with the likes of Tennessee, LSU, Duke, defending National Champion Maryland and North Carolina out there as competition.

The early part of the season wasn't terribly challenging as UConn easily defeated Richmond, Colgate and Boston University, all at home. Houston excelled in all those games and had 20 points and 9 rebounds against Richmond. Charles and Hunter had double-doubles against Colgate and Thomas led all scorers with 14 points against Boston University as she posted a perfect 4-4 shooting performance from beyond the arch. The Huskies didn't play a difficult early season schedule and that may have come back to haunt them at the end of the season.

UConn faced its first test of the season when it faced no. 9 Purdue on November 30 at Gampel. UConn improved to 4-0 for the tenth time in the last 11 seasons with a hard fought 66-55 win. Purdue led for the first 12 minutes of the first half as both teams played tight defense.

After the Purdue win the Huskies went on an 8 game winning streak in which no team came closer than 19 points. Perhaps the key game during that stretch was at West Virginia on January 2. West Virginia had made it to the Big East finals the year before at the Hartford Civic Center after upsetting a highly favored Rutgers team. They gave UConn fits before losing the chance to get an NCAA bid.

The Mountaineers led early on and hit a three pointer with 11:36 on the clock to take their last lead at 14-13. The Huskies closed the first half with a 25-5 run over the final 7:35 to take a 16 point half time advantage at the very difficult West Virginia Coliseum.

UConn controlled the game in the second half and ended up winning 63-44.

Charles led the charge of three players in double figures with her second consecutive double-double with 16 points and 12 rebounds. Houston continued her stellar play with 16 points and 9 rebounds.

With the win UConn opened the season at 12-0 for the first time since 2002-03 and the eighth time since 1996-97 and extended its winning streak against West Virginia to 18 consecutive games.

Next up for the Huskies was the highly anticipated match up with Tennessee at a sold out and very boisterous Hartford Civic Center. Tennessee was ranked no. 5 in the country and UConn was ranked no. 6 at the time. There was a national television audience watching on CBS.

Charles had a good first half but the Lady Vols led throughout and went into the locker-room at half time leading 41-29. The 41 points scored by Tennessee marked the most points scored by a UConn opponent that season and was the first time that the Huskies trailed at half time.

Tennessee opened the second half on a 6-0 run which was highlighted by a dunk by sophomore player of the year candidate Candace Parker. That dunk on their home court seemed to ignite UConn as they went on a furious rally to knot the score at 58 on a Thomas trey from the corner with 4:48 left on the clock. Tennessee then went on a mini run and with 23 seconds left in the game Houston scored to get the Huskies within three at 67-64. Alexis Hornbuckle of Tennessee sealed the game with two free throws for a scintillating 70-64 win.

The key to the game for the Huskies was the emergence of an injured Hunter who played a full 19 minutes and excelled defensively against Parker. No one obviously wanted to be the Huskies opponent after Tennessee and unfortunately for Seton Hall they became a 48 point victim at Gampel as UConn scored over 100 points for the first time during the season. Syracuse then fell by 31 points two days before Martin Luther King Day in a date with number 2 North Carolina on the road on national television.

After the rout of Syracuse, UConn only had two turn around days before facing number 2 North Carolina on Martin Luther King Day on national television. UConn had become a staple on national television on ESPN on Martin Luther

King Day which led many to ask whether or not Martin Luther King was actually a graduate of the University of Connecticut.

Carolina opened a quick 14-6 lead, but the Huskies led by Montgomery and Hunter cut it to 34-33.

North Carolina held the 5 point half time lead despite committing 20 turnovers in the opening twenty minutes.

Carolina went on a 10-2 run to open the second half and to garner a 60-45 lead. In a game of runs the Huskies then went on a 25-10 run keyed by sophomore Kalana Greene to knot the game at 68-68.

North Carolina battled back to reclaim the lead with a three pointer by their star, Ivory Latta which led ultimately to an 82-76 victory in Chapel Hill, North Carolina.

Auriemma was happy with the Huskies progress and felt that at least in the second half they had played probably their most complete half of the season. He waited anxiously for his team to put together two sold halves against the top 25 team.

Neither a vastly improved Providence nor St. John's offered any of that opposition. Providence fell by 43 in their first game ever at the Duncan Donuts Center in downtown Providence and the Huskies had an opportunity to play at Madison Square Garden against St. John's. That was always one of Auriemma's dreams both as a player and a coach and his team won by 21 points. On the Saturday night before the game he took them to see the Color Purple and to a fine New York steak house. It was experience that neither he nor his players will ever forget.

The Huskies were then tested by DePaul at Gampel. UConn was up for most of the game but DePaul fought back to make it a five point game with 2:05 to go but Houston answered back with a jumper to give UConn a 78-71 lead and the Huskies closed out the game with a 10-5 run to account for the final margin of twelve. Greene had her third double double of the season with a career high 25 points and 12 rebounds.

Next game Notre Dame and head coach Muffet McGraw, a good friend of Auriemma's. A much improved Notre Dame team fell tamely at Gampel by 17 and then the Huskies faced, unexpectedly their toughest Big East test to date.

UConn traveled to Cincinnati on January 30 for a Mel Thomas homecoming of sorts and faced, unexpectedly their toughest Big East challenge to date. Cincinnati was not very heralded going into the game at 3-5 in Conference.

The Bearcats jumped out to a 6-0 lead to begin the contest and then the lead swung back and forth with Cincy grabbing a 60-59 lead with five minutes to go. Montgomery drained a jumper just inside the top of the key with 59 seconds remaining to cap a late 7-0 run that put the Huskies up for good at 66-60 as they outscored Cincinnati 15-2 in the final 5:05. Houston played the first 4 minutes of the game and then was benched by Auriemma largely as a result of what he deemed to be her lackluster play. Most in attendance knew that she really had to step up her effort if she was to see significant minutes in key upcoming Big East contests against Marquette and Rutgers.

The Huskies traveled to Milwaukee to take on No. 16 Marquette. Charles had her seventh double-double this season with a season high 20 points and 14 rebounds as UConn held off a late second half surge for Marquette for a 52-48 win to improve the Huskies to 20-2 on the season and stay a perfect 10-0 in the Big East. The win marked the 14th consecutive season and the 18th time in Program's history that UConn had won 20 games in a season.

UConn limited Marquette to its lowest point total in any half this season as it held the Golden Eagles to 24 staff points.

Marquette closed to within 50-48 with 35 seconds remaining on a 5-0 run but with 11.1 seconds remaining Montgomery knocked down two free throws for the win.

Next up for UConn was a home contest against Big East arch rival enigmatic, Rutgers. Auriemma has said on a number of occasions both on and off the record that Rutgers is the team he most likes to beat. He entered that February 6 game coming off of an uncharacteristic three game losing streak against the Scarlet Knights.

In many of the UConn-Rutgers games, especially in Connecticut, UConn has traditionally jumped off to big leads and the February contest was no different. UConn led 25-10 before all the fans were in their seats in Storrs. Rutgers was tentative in their strength, their 55 defense wasn't working. Freshman star Epiphanny Prince did not score in the first half and Swanier and Montgomery provided, in addition to Charles most of the first half offense. UConn took a 30-23 lead into the half time break.

UConn opened the second half on an 11-0 run and Connecticut would not allow Rutgers to get any closer than 9 points with less than two minutes remaining as the Huskies held on to win 60-50. Many thought that the Scarlett Knights would be hard pressed to beat UConn at any point and time during the season, especially during the Big East Tournament at Hartford.

The Huskies then drilled a ranked Louisville team at Gampel 84-56 behind 20 points from Montgomery. Pittsburgh put up some what of a challenge in the second half at the Hartford Civic Center but fell 82-68 on a day in which Shea Ralph returned to Connecticut and was presented with her Wall of Fame plaque by Auriemma and Athletic Director Jeff Hathaway. Besides that Pittsburgh had little to cheer about as it related to their performance on the court. Connecticut easily defeated a good South Florida team on the road 81-67 and then blew out Villanova 92-49 at the Hartford Civic Center. Auriemma is a good friend of Villanova head coach Peretta and if that wasn't the case UConn easily could have won by eighty points. The UConn starters were out of the game well before the end of forty minutes.

Next game was the rematch at Rutgers and many of the scribes indicated that Rutgers should be able to beat UConn at the Rutgers Athletic Center with their huge crowd and home court advantage, despite the ten point loss at Gampel earlier in the season. Auriemma helped to antagonize the situation by making a negative comment about Rutgers fans as a whole, calling them "miserable." He then amended that by saying that only 10% of the Rutgers fans are miserable and 90% of them are probably good solid basketball fans.

Auriemma, as he had done previously with Duke and Tennessee in prior seasons managed to get into the heads of the Rutgers fans through the media before the game and that along with his team's stellar play to start the game basically created a RAC in which the 100 or so UConn fans were making more noise than the 7,000 highly partisan Rutgers fans. UConn easily won 70-44 keyed by Montgomery's 21 points. Thomas dropped in 16 points for her 14th game in double figures and Houston added 11 and the win. UConn finished the season with an undefeated Big East Conference record at 16-0 for the first time since 2003 and the sixth time in the Program's history.

The game left Rutgers head coach Vivian Stringer scratching her head. She knew that something was drastically wrong with her teams' play against UConn but she couldn't quite put her finger on it. It was especially evident on the offensive end.

The Big East Tournament was next at the not quite so neutral Hartford Civic Center. The Huskies opened up with South Florida and won on Sunday after receiving a bye in the first round. They were paced by Houston's 22 points and Charles, both of whom registered a double-double. The Bulls dropped to 20-11 and a great deal of insecurity about whether or not they would get an NCAA bid. They ultimately did not get one.

Next came Louisville, the no. 23 ranked team in the country and after Louisville scored the first 5 points of the game UConn responded with a 14-2 run. UConn never looked back and held an 18 point lead at the half. Montgomery and Greene combined for 26 first half points, outscoring Louisville by themselves in the first half. UConn went on for a 76-50 victory.

The Big East Player of the Year, Louisville's Angel McCoughtry was held to a season low 9 points and the UConn crowd booed when she came out. Auriemma did not take offense at that, saying instead that she should have been booed because "she stunk." Many questioned that comment.

The UConn win set up the third meeting with Rutgers who had defeated both DePaul and Marquette to make it into the Big East finals. Auriemma was confident in going into the game as were his players.

What UConn saw though in front of 9,000 fans was a far different Rutgers team and a game that would catapult Rutgers into national prominence and ultimately into the National Championship game against Tennessee in Cleveland in early April.

Rutgers led by three at the half but UConn used a 9-0 swing to take a 5 point lead. Rutgers regained the lead at 49-45 and UConn was held without a field goal for the last 7:38 of the second half, missing its last ten field goal attempts before connecting with 18 seconds left to end the drought.

Rutgers played tenacious defense and had a number of steals and really caught UConn off guard.

After the game, Auriemma minimized the loss and when talking about his team's play said "we sucked." He did little to compliment Rutgers.

After the Rutgers loss UConn had to wait a week for selection Monday. Auriemma gave his team three days off and they had a couple of very good practices before their sites were announced on national television. Auriemma felt satisfied that his team had put the Rutgers loss behind it and was focusing on the upcoming NCAA Tournament.

The Huskies gathered together with Auriemma and received the news immediately on ESPN that they would be a no. 1 seed and would be sent to the Fresno region. Taking a look at the other regions this was certainly good news for UConn despite the fact that they probably fell to the fourth number 1 seed after the Rutgers loss.

Their two opening games in Hartford figured to be easy against UMBC and probably Wisconsin-Green Bay.

Many of the writers who cover UConn felt right after the Selection Show that the most difficult hurdle for UConn in the Fresno bracket before reaching the Final Four in Cleveland would be NC State. This was an emotional NC State team which had won the ACC Tournament and in the process had beaten both Duke and North Carolina. Their veteran coach, Kay Yow was suffering from cancer and many felt that this would be her last season. There would certainly be an emotional component to that game and Auriemma had it circled on his calendar.

UConn opened the Tournament by completely dominating UNBC 82-33 in Hartford. It was the fewest points allowed by a UConn team in an NCAA Tournament game since 2001.

UConn went on one of its patented runs at the end of the first half and into the second half, outscoring UNBC 21-0. The 49 point win by UConn marked the largest margin of victory in the NCAA Tournament for the Huskies since defeating St. Francis (Pa) by an identical 49 point margin in 2002.

Montgomery paced the way with a game high 19 points to lead five players in double figures. Clearly balance was the key word for UConn as it had been all season.

And off it was to the Sweet Sixteen as UConn overcame a 40-38 half time deficit to UW-Green Bay and in the process snapped their 28 game winning streak 94-70 to advance to the Sweet Sixteen in the NCAA Tournament. Charles scored 22 points and Thomas had 21. With the win, UConn has now won 14 consecutive NCAA second round games and advance to the NCAA Regional semi-finals for the 14th consecutive time. Houston, Montgomery and Greene each brought in 16 points in the victory.

The Huskies entered the NCAA Tournament with a 29-3 record and many felt that they had the easiest path to Cleveland in the Final Four. They would play their first two games at home at the Hartford Civic Center and then have to travel to Fresno, the first time in the history of the Program that they had been sent out west, having to defeat presumably North Carolina State and Stanford to make it to the Final Four.

The Huskies opened the quest with an 82-33 route of University of Maryland-Baltimore County. UConn held UNBC without a single point during a 21-0 run in the first half to close out the game. With the victory UConn advanced to the second round of the NCAA Tournament for the 14 consecutive season. The Huskies next faced University of Wisconsin at Green Ban. Fueled by freshman Tina Charles' 22 points and Thomas' 21 points, Connecticut snapped Green Bay's national best 26 game winning streak 94-70 to advance to the Sweet Sixteen. Green Bay took a 40-38 edge into the locker room at half time but UConn opened the second half on a 15-2 run to take a 62-50 lead and the game was for all practical purposes over.

The Huskies flew out to Fresno and played a very emotional game against North Carolina State. Kay Yow is and has been suffering from cancer and has always been a friend of Auriemma's. He greatly respects her both on and off the bench and he joked before the game that many of his family would probably be rooting for her over him.

UConn though was all business when they took the court and despite falling behind on numerous occasions against the no. 4 seed they defeated State 78-71 at the Save Mart Center to advance to the Elite Eight. Houston led all scorers with 18 points. Greene registered her fifth double-double of the season with 17 points and 12 rebounds. Auriemma had a very poignant conversation with Yow at the end of the game on the sidelines.

Stanford got knocked out of the Tournament earlier and UConn had to play yet another emotional and this time re-match game two days later against LSU. A scandal had hit the LSU campus a few weeks before and head coach Pokey Chatman was forced to resign. Long time assistant Bob Starkey took over the team and fielded the same squad that UConn had defeated earlier in the season on LSU's difficult home court.

The Tigers opened up a 16-10 lead early in the game. The Huskies cut LSU's lead to 7 after Montgomery knocked down a three pointer but the Tigers then used a 10-0 run to extent their lead to 17 at 34-17. The Tigers led 34-22 at the half marking UConn's lowest scoring output for a first half this season.

LSU went on another run to open the second half but Thomas nailed a three pointer to cut the deficit to 50-38.

LSU then controlled the game for the rest of the second half, hitting 10-11 from the charity stripe to take the game 73-50. Their star an All-American player Sylvia Fowles had a double-double with 23 points and 15 rebounds. The loss marked UConn's largest margin of defeat in an NCAA Tournament game since 1992 when they lost to Vanderbilt 75-47.

Auriemma had to look at a Final Four with arch rivals Tennessee and Rutgers along with LSU and North Carolina. During the Tournament there was much speculation fueled in Connecticut that Auriemma was drawing interest from the University of Florida to replace deposed coach Carolyn Peck. After a few days of uncertainty in late March, Auriemma denied the rumors and noted that he was staying in Connecticut. Sources close to the Program indicated that Auriemma would never leave for another women's job but could leave some day if the right men's job came along. There were rumors the previous season that the men's job at Oklahoma had been offered to Auriemma and he found it quite attractive but was not willing to leave Connecticut until his son Mike graduated from high school.

Some of the publications had Tennessee ranked preseason no. 1 despite the fact that Maryland, the defending national champions returned all five starters. Tennessee returned the consensus National Player of the Year in Candace Parker, a 6'4" sophomore center who could also play the forward and guard positions along with her well known ability to dunk the ball. Tennessee also returned sweet shooting senior Sidney Spencer, a 6'3" forward from Alabama, guard Alexis

Hornbuckle, junior forward Nicky Anosike and brought in 5'4" freshman guard Kait McMahon from Maryville, Tennessee.

Summitt calls it tradition and the names on the jerseys. She recognizes that there are other teams in the country that have more talent than Tennessee and UConn this year but that both teams step onto the court each night "expecting to win". She was not surprised that both teams ended up being number one seeds in the Tournament.

The Lady Vols then hosted UCLA at home and cruised to an 83-60 victory playing a more uptempo style. Parker scored 22 points and Spencer added 15. After the game Summitt noted that "Candace scored a lot of different ways as she always does." That showed the versatility of Parker.

Tennessee next traveled to play a very tough Arizona State team on the road. Parker's double-double led the Lady Vols past Arizona State 83-74 in a game in which Tennessee only led by 4 at the half.

Tennessee then took on a potential Final Four team in traditional rival Stanford at home and won by 17, 77-60. Parker had 25 points and after the game Summitt noted that "without a doubt, I thought this was her best all-around game." Tennessee was clearly one of the top teams in the nation and moved into the number 4 spot after the win.

Summitt's team then blew out Middle Tennessee at home by 24 and had an easy 21 point win against traditional rival Louisville Tech on the road. That led to a road show down against number 2 North Carolina.

Despite 24 points by Candace Parker Tennessee fell 72-57 in a rematch of last year's regional final. North Carolina led narrowly at the half by 5 but opened up a much larger lead in the second half. The key stat was rebounding in which the Lady Vols, normally one of the top rebounding teams in the country were out rebounded 43-33. Erlana Larkins led North Carolina with 17 points and 12 rebounds in 37 minutes of play.

Tennessee then got back to its winning ways with a 56 point win over Summitt's alma mater, Tennessee Martin. They then beat a George Washington team by 23 points behind Spencer's 21 points. George Washington would later go on to become the number 9 team in the country.

Tennessee then traveled to Austin, Texas and took on Texas for the 30th consecutive year. The Texas basketball fortunes have been down for many years and Tennessee had no trouble with a 21 point win. Summitt noted after the game that as most Tennessee-Texas games it was very intense and once again made Summitt think why her team plays the tough schedule that it does but she noted that "we do it to get to post-season."

Tennessee then played a rare game against West Virginia and had a real struggle with the Mountaineers before beating them 66-51 behind Parker's 19 points and 25 minutes.

Notre Dame and Alabama both fell tamely at Knoxville by the counts of 78-54 and 72-36 setting up a January 6, 2007 meeting with Connecticut on the road.

Summitt's team was primed for the game despite the huge Connecticut throng in the Civic Center. They arrived in Hartford on Thursday before the game and originally had scheduled a practice for the University of Hartford. Hartford is coached by former UConn star Jen Rizzotti and for some reason Tennessee switched it's practice to earlier in the day at Trinity College. Many media members did not get notice of this switch and hence didn't have as much access as desired to the Tennessee coaching staff and players.

The night before the game Summitt, some of her assistant coaches and a group of Tennessee boosters had dinner at a famous Hartford establishment, Trumbull Kitchen. Diners at the restaurant were a bit stunned when Summitt walked in and many mistook her for her sister who was also on the trip up east.

Game day for some reason didn't feel like a typical UConn-Tennessee clash, at least from the perspective of the crowd waiting to enter the Hartford Civic Center at 3:00 p.m. for a 4:00 p.m. CBS national television game. Perhaps it was a function of the fact that neither Tennessee nor UConn were number one or two in the country but for whatever reason it felt more like a mundane Big East game than UConn-Tennessee.

Tennessee got off to a big lead in the first half behind Candice Parker and was up by as many as 19 in the second half when Parker decided to dunk on a breakaway lay up. This ignited the UConn crowd and team and Auriemma's squad came back to tie the game in the last seven minutes. They never took the lead and Tennessee held on for a narrow victory and a happy trip back to Knoxville on a chartered plane.

Tennessee next faced no. 1 Duke at home and the Blue Devils demonstrated why at the time they were the top team in the country easily handling Tennessee with their suffocating defense. What was interesting about the game is that Tennessee men's coach Bruce Pearl sat in the student section and had his face and body painted in Tennessee colors. A national television audience caught this and many in the know knew that it was just a matter of time until Summitt reciprocated.

The Tennessee men faced Florida at home in late February and there was a buzz around college basketball that Summitt would show up and try to emulate the antics of Pearl. Well truth be told Summitt outdid him. At the 16:00 media timeout in the first half, Summitt and her assistants were escorted on to the court shrouded in camouflage all wearing Tennessee cheerleading outfits. Summitt opened up the Program by singing Rocky Top to the crowd and the national television audience, and they led the cheerleaders in a cheer standing on their shoulders. That drew an ovation. The Tennessee men actually knocked off no. 1 Florida that night.

Vanderbilt provided some opposition for Tennessee on the road but Spencer came through with 26 points on strong outside shooting and Parker recorded yet another double-double as Tennessee pulled away in the second half for a 10 point win. In mid-February Tennessee traveled to LSU and it was a nip and tuck game most of the way but Parker's inside-outside game and more importantly her 27 points and 13 rebounds caused Tennessee to hold off a late rallying and no. 7 ranked LSU by 5, 56-51.

Tennessee opened up the SEC Tournament with an easy 18 point win over South Carolina and Marciniak but then fell on March 3 in the semi-finals to LSU 63-54 despite a career high 29 points by Hornbuckle. Sylvia Fowles scored 19 points and had 20 rebounds for LSU and Tennessee star Parker was held to 4 points. The Lady Vols lost their first Conference game since falling to Florida on February 26, 2006.

Tennessee had a difficult Region in the NCAA Tournament but it provided less opposition than many had previously thought due to some upsets. Tennessee opened up the Tournament with an easy win over Drake in Pittsburgh and then beat the host school, University of Pittsburgh by 14.

They next faced tiny Marist who came into the game with two huge upset victories. Tennessee was never headed by the smaller New York school and won easily 65-46.

Mississippi was next and Ole Miss was playing perhaps the best basketball in the country at the time especially after an easy win in Hartford over heavily favored Maryland.

Parker dominated at both ends of the court and the Lady Vols got contributions from almost everyone on the roster as they rolled to a 98-62 victory in Dayton. Star guard Armintie Price from Mississippi had her usual big game with 30 points but no one else was a factor as Tennessee rolled to their 17th Final Four under Summitt.

Mississippi's Carol Ross was certainly awe inspired by the Tennessee performance and noted that "Pat is the best at getting her team to post season play, she always has them ready to go."

The win set up a match-up with North Carolina in the National semis in Cleveland, a team that had defeated Tennessee in the Elite Eight the year before also in Cleveland and had defeated Tennessee earlier in December when Tennessee played one of its weakest defensive games of the year.

The stage was set in Cleveland and the stands were full of Lady Vol orange. Tennessee outnumbered the combined fan base of Rutgers, LSU and North Carolina at the Final Four. Everyone in Cleveland one could see orange, even at the Rock & Roll Hall of Fame for their numerous Final Four related events.

The Tennessee fans came out in droves for the open practices on Saturday and gave their team a thundering ovation.

Tennessee took the court at prime time on Sunday night after Rutgers had dismantled LSU.

The game certainly didn't go the way Tennessee had wanted as Tennessee was down most of the game and North Carolina held a commanding 48-36 lead with 8:18 to play. At that point Anosikie and Parker went on a Tar for Tennessee and fueled by a 14-2 run tied the Tar Heels at 50-all.

Tennessee then scored the final 6 points of the game to win 56-50, eerily reminiscent of the Tar Heels collapse against Georgetown in the men's Elite Eight at the Meadowlands one week before.

For the Tar Heels last 15 possessions they scored just 2 points and missed all 8 field goal attempts.

Parker finished with 14 points and 13 rebounds, yet another double-double and Anosikie added 14 points.

Tennessee celebrated at the end of the game but it was clear that the mission was not over. There was one more game remaining and Parker made that clear to the highly partisan crowd as she left the court with her finger up, not in a victory celebration but pointing towards one more game. Summitt did the same thing verbally to many in the crowd. This was not born from arrogance, but born from a desire to not finish second but win another National Championship in a year in which perhaps they weren't even favored to make it to the Final Four.

Next came Rutgers on a stage for two of the winningest coaches in women's basketball history, C. Vivian Stringer and Summitt. They are very close friends and there was obviously no sub plot about Vivian and Pat going into the game. It was all about their teams.

Rutgers was on a high and probably playing the best basketball of any team in the country at the time. They completely bottled up the star of all opposing teams with their patented "55" defense and most recently had held Sylvia Fowles of LSU to only 5 points and few rebounds. It was felt by some commentators that they would do the same to Parker and Stacey Dales of ESPN actually picked Rutgers to win.

The betting line in Las Vegas had Rutgers as a 3 point underdog and no one really knew what to expect going into the game.

Call the National Championship game offensive rebounding because that is what it was about.

Rutgers went off on an early 8-6 lead but that would be really the end for the Scarlet Knights. They were tentative throughout, unlike their other appearances and seemed to be playing like freshman. Well freshman they were with five playing a major role on this team.

The key stat in the game was as previously mentioned offensive rebounds. Rutgers had 14 and Tennessee had 24. Tennessee out rebounded Rutgers 42-34 and it seemed like much more than that. Anosikie had an amazing 16 rebounds, including 10 on the offensive glass and Parker had 17 points and Bobbitt had 13 on 4-8 shooting from 3 point land. Sidney Spencer added 11 and Alberta August came off the bench for 15 minutes of play and added 10 points and 5 rebounds.

The Tennessee defense put the clamps on Rutgers' star Matee Ajavon, holding her to 8 points on 3-9 shooting and only two 3 point makes. The entire Rutgers team only made two 3 pointers while they made 8-10 in the first half against LSU.

Rocky Top and confetti were evident as soon as the final horn sounded throughout the arena in Cleveland.

While Tennessee won its seventh National Championship in 2007, Connecticut obviously had a season that was fulfilling in many ways, but as previously detailed ended in disappointment.

The Huskies of 2006-07 didn't have the star power that they've had in the past. There wasn't a Rizzotti, Lobo, Wolters, Sales, Ralph, Abrosimova, Bird, Jones, Williams, Cash or Taurasi to capture the fancy of the fandom. Perhaps that's a reason that very few of their home games at the Hartford Civil Center were sell-outs.

That might change soon, though. Center Tina Charles, despite her worst game of the season in Fresno against LSU appears to be a star in the making. Charde Houston, Renee Montgomery and Kalana Greene all improved their games throughout the season.

But the big question for the Huskies of 06-07 was … two minutes left, tie game and where is the ball going? It's only a rather critical basketball question.

And for years in many outposts, the answers have been obvious throughout the game. Give it to Larry. Give it to M.J. Give it to Kareem.

At UConn, the answers have been equally obvious. Give it to Nykesha. Give it to Diana. Give it to Sue. Clearly, the answers were clearer before 2007.

Two minutes left, tie game and do you give it to Houston? Mel Thomas? Charles? Brittany Hunter? Montgomery?

The best answer Auriemma could muster at various points of the season was, "It depends."

When a writer informed Auriemma that "it depends" is the wrong answer, he chuckled.

"Hey," he said. "Joe Montana isn't taking a snap anymore. Elvis has left the building. You see where each game takes you."

And maybe that's the primary difference between the pre-Diana and post-Diana Huskies. Since Diana's departure, UConn has played its best only when a "give me the ball and get out of the way" player emerged: Barbara Turner in last year's NCAA Tournament, for instance.

The offense this season, while quite capable, just doesn't have the Nykesha, Kara, Shea, Svet, Swin, Asjha, Diana, Sue or even Barbara of last March, who provided fans and media with a sense of calm in late-game situations.

Meanwhile, in other parts of the country …

Tennessee gave it to Candace Parker.

Maryland had a number of options, primarily Crystal Langhorne (although Kristi Toliver, Shay Doron, Marissa Coleman and Laura Harper weren't bad either).

Duke had Lindsey Harding, Abby Waner and Alison Bales.

Carolina had Ivory Latta.

Rutgers had Ajavon and Carson.

And UConn fans were worried about giving it to Houston, who might travel. Sure, that's fatalistic.

But it's also somewhat realistic, even if it's in a fatalistic sort of way.

"This team is better in transition," Auriemma said after a win over DePaul in midseason, adding that the Huskies of '07 don't have the same passing skills as teams of the past.

Translation: Half-court offense, which the women once ran with the smoothness of Miles Davis and his trumpet, isn't the surest bet in sports anymore.

"We're not very sophisticated on offense," Auriemma said. "There were days when we could say, 'This is what we're going to do and there's nothing you can do about it. Now, there's a pretty good chance we'll need Plan B."

If nothing else, the need for Plan B all these years later indicates the degree of basketball fantasyland Auriemma once provided. The Huskies suddenly have the same issues as most other schools in the country. Auriemma's friends in coaching like to call him and revel in how he has to worry about what everybody else has to worry about.

This isn't necessarily a bad thing. It made the games more exciting and less predictable. Auriemma could chuckle when it was suggested to him that "this is why he makes the big bucks." He liked the challenge. Although the Real Geno is probably best illustrated through a quote he once had about being picked behind Rutgers.

"I like being the favorite," he said. "People asked me before (last) season, 'Won't this be exciting with no All-Americans and no superstars? Aren't you looking forward to it? I said, 'Hell no.' It's like going to a poker game with 20 bucks and getting (lousy) cards. I want the biggest pile and the best cards. I want the best players. I want to be ranked No. 1. Then I want to kick everybody else's butt."

Auriemma had a very interesting season. In September, he was inducted into the Naismith Memorial Basketball Hall of Fame. He coached his team well, as usual, getting it to the Elite Eight. But perhaps he was filled with the most pride was watching his son, Michael, play basketball at East Catholic of Manchester.

Mike Auriemma was a senior, who led East Catholic to a conference title and to the state championship game. One of Mike's state tournament games came during the night his dad's team played in the Big East Tournament semifinals against Louisville. His postgame comments provided a look inside at who he really is.

That night, Auriemma admitted at times, he was an out-of-place dad, whose thoughts were elsewhere, like with his son.

"His high school career could have ended tonight," Geno said, happily knowing that it didn't. East Catholic won its first-round state tournament game. When

Geno met reporters, however, he didn't know the score of the East Catholic game. It was only after the formal news conference that he learned it was 46-42 East with a few minutes left. How did he get the score? Athletic director Jeff Hathaway phoned his wife, who was at the East Catholic game, not the UConn game. Hathaway relayed the score. So much for UConn-Louisville being the biggest sporting event in Connecticut that night.

Why was Mrs. Hathaway so interested? The Hathaways have a daughter at East Catholic. So does UConn football coach Randy Edsall, making East Catholic a rather noteworthy high school.

It wasn't until Geno had gabbed for a few minutes that Randy Press of UConn sports communications announced that East was up by 12 with 12 seconds left.

"Now we're talking," Geno said. "I can smile."

And then the Geno most of you never see, Geno the dad, started talking.

"I was thinking about it a lot," he said, referring to Mike's game. "Coming out at halftime I was wondering how they were doing. It was 7 o'clock and they hadn't even started yet…. I didn't want his high school career to come to an end without me there." Auriemma has been a sports-watching parent before. His older daughter, Jenna, played basketball at Manchester High several years ago. One night when Manchester was at NFA, Auriemma was watching Jenna play and cracked, "She may be short. But you know what? She's slow."

This is different. Mike Auriemma is going to be a Division I player, headed to prep school next year. Watching Mike play was as rewarding, if not more, than the five national championships.

"I watch him from the same standpoint that I did Diana (Taurasi) and Sveta (Abrosimova)," Geno said. "When I watched them play, I was emotionally interested in those two for some reason. Everything they did early on wasn't good enough, no matter what. As they got older, they could do no wrong.

"I'll tell him, 'You gotta make free throws more. You're a coach's kid. You're making me look bad,'" Geno said.

"Before he got to East Catholic, I'd ask, 'How come you don't dive on more loose balls?'" Geno said. "He says, 'I'm not a loose-ball-diving kind of guy.' I told Luke

(East Catholic coach Luke Reilly) that if he got him to take a charge at East, I'd write a blank check.

"How about his first varsity game? I'll never forget it. I think it was at Berlin. Charge. I was dumbfounded."

Did he ever write the check?

"No," Geno said. "Anybody can do it once. You know what his total charges are in his high school career? One."

The night illustrated how coaches are fathers, too, sometimes, who sit there and watch and root and get nervous.

Mike's season had been over for a few weeks when the team went to Fresno for the regional. After UConn defeated North Carolina State, it was to play LSU in the regional final, for the right to go to the Final Four.

There was Auriemma, a day earlier, answering questions about his program's "mystique" and the significance of the name "Connecticut" across the front of the uniform. The rest of the world, right to tip-off of the LSU game, was still viewing the UConn women as the Yankees and the Gatsbys of women's college basketball. There was good reason for that. You don't dismiss history and pedigree.

But the history belonged more to LSU than Connecticut. It was the LSU players who had been to three straight Final Fours, not Connecticut. That means the Lady Tigers had gone 3-for-3 in the game many coaches think is the hardest to win in the tournament.

The Lady Tigers also had one other thing going for them: The sheriff in the middle. Sylvia Fowles, who had 22 points and 17 rebounds the last time the teams played in Baton Rouge, was even better Monday, when LSU tap-danced on UConn, all the way to Cleveland.

Clearly, the combination of The Sheriff's 23 points and 15 rebounds and LSU's experience was way too much for the Huskies, who turned in an absolute stinkeroo at the worst possible moment. And nobody really saw it coming. Interim LSU coach Bob Starkey said Sunday he thought LSU played well against UConn in Baton Rouge—and UConn still won.

"We can't win unless they help us out," he said.

Starkey, a nice enough fellow, doesn't have any Lou Holtz in him. He really believed LSU playing well wouldn't be enough. UConn had to turn in no better than a C minus.

The Huskies obliged with an 'F.' Were they timid? At times. And a little overwhelmed by Fowles, the biggest thing in purple since Barney. And when Fowles wasn't inhaling everything in her path, Allison Hightower and Ashley Thomas went 5-for-6 shooting 3s, a neat trick for two players who had gone 23-for-84 during the season.

This was the kind of game that proved why coaches don't sleep. They lay awake in fear of the other team doing everything right and their team doing everything wrong.

When the teams played during the regular season, Charles scored 17 points and at least somewhat neutralized Fowles' effectiveness. Charles, who deserves all the hosannas for an outstanding freshman season, pulled a no-show. She was UConn's most important player in the game. She scored one point.

Houston, who also came a long way this season, wasn't much better. She scored four.

Charles went scoreless in the first half and was sent to the bench early in the second. She didn't return until 8 minutes, 9 seconds remained and the game all but decided.

UConn guard Renee Montgomery had no idea how prophetic she sounded a day earlier when she was asked about UConn's mystique.

"We're not a dynasty anymore," Montgomery said.

Nobody in a UConn uniform for the next season, just as nobody was this season, will have played at the Final Four.

"The name on the front of the uniform means different things and different times, depending on who's wearing the jersey," Auriemma said. "I think there's a little bit of mystique with the success we've had and how the kids embrace it. I just don't know if we scare anybody."

"We came a long way and in a lot of ways we overachieved," Auriemma said. "But when you get a game from the Final Four ... LSU exposed all the things we're not good at."

Interviews were over and team was about to leave for the airport. In the hallway of Save Mart Center stood Kathy Auriemma, who is as insightful as her husband. Kathy managed to find some perspective.

"They've all suffered," Kathy said. "There hasn't been one championship team here that hasn't."

It was only the perfect use of the word.

Because not only does it provide an abridged history of the program, it also illustrates that the brand of suffering at UConn is a little different than in other places.

Kathy Auriemma meant this: All five national championship teams at UConn endured bitter disappointment in the NCAA Tournament before hanging the banner.

It took Rebecca Lobo until her senior year to make the Final Four. It took Jennifer Rizzotti and Jamelle Elliot three years. The Lobo/Rizzotti/Elliot years featured a first-round loss to Louisville and an Elite Eight loss to North Carolina, every bit as depressing as the loss to LSU.

The 2000 team was the first Connecticut outfit to make the Final Four in four years. The Shea/Svet team went out in the Elite Eight in 1997 and 98 and then to Iowa State in the Sweet 16 in 1999. UConn was the favorite in all three losses, injuries to Ralph and Sales not withstanding.

The undefeated team of 2002 used the angst of a blown 15-point lead against Notre Dame in the 2001 Final Four as its primary fuel. It is doubtful the 2002 team, with Bird, Williams, Jones, Cash and Taurasi, would have gone undefeated had the sting of the '01 national semifinal not caused so much heartburn.

And while Ann Strother and Barbara Turner won two straight titles as underclassmen, they certainly suffered later in their careers. They went out against Stanford in the 2005 Sweet 16 and last season in a very difficult loss to Duke in overtime.

So now we have the newbies, who are probably going to win one before they leave. And what happened Monday would just make it sweeter for Montgomery, Charles and Houston. No, it's not going to be a particularly fun offseason, because the aftertaste of LSU will be worse than cough medicine, lingering into the summer months.

It's somewhat comical, though, that we're even using the word "suffering," accurate as it is. In most programs, "suffering" entails losing seasons, lost recruits or killer injuries. In most programs, a 32-4 season would be cause for a parade. In Connecticut, it's cause for grief counseling.

It's not easy to encapsulate what the Huskies accomplished this season. There was plenty of good: a Big East regular season championship, 32 wins, and steady improvement of nearly all the primary players. If Houston, Charles, Montgomery, Ketia Swanier and the rest improve as steadily again, the addition of promising recruit Maya Moore should be enough to get the Huskies to Tampa, site of the 2008 Final Four.

But there was some bad, too. They lost to Tennessee and Carolina during the regular season. They lost the Big East Tournament final to Rutgers. And they lost in the Elite Eight. An argument could be made that they lost the four biggest games of the season.

That's what happens when you make eight Final Fours and win five National Championships since 1985. Anything less is cause for a "yeah, but." Indeed, Auriemma has more than Italian heritage and mondo championships with Joe Torre, the oft criticized but highly successful manager of the Yankees. Regular season success, certainly significant, becomes irrelevant under the weight of postseason failure. Especially when the entire State of Connecticut and most of the nation is watching either in person or on television.

But don't feel too badly for Auriemma. He is one of the favorites to win a National Championship in 2007-2008 and will have within the next year three National Players of the Year on this squad. Not bad for someone who hasn't won a championship since Taurasi.

THE PLAYERS

Great players have played in the UConn-Tennessee series over the years. Some of the greatest in women's college basketball history. A team of all UConn-Tennessee players would have won the National Championship in any year. Some of the greatest players ever to play in the series either didn't play in enough games to make our list, were injured or didn't have great games in that series but did in their college and pro careers. We hate to leave out the likes of Rebecca Lobo, Kara Wolters, Tamika Catchings, Svetlana Abrosimova, Nykesha Sales and Swin Cash. But after careful consideration and analysis along with interviews with coaches and players throughout the country, Shea Ralph, Sue Bird, Chamique Holdsclaw, Semeka Randall and of course the best of them all Diana Taurasi had career game(s) on this the biggest stage in women's college basketball, both regular season and in NCAA games. We have also left out without naming them the one game wonders who had great single games in the series but didn't follow them up with one or two more in their careers against this foe. It is our intention to start with the best of all these players in the series, Taurasi and then consider the other four on a relatively equal basis.

Has anyone ever captured a state and indeed a nation of women's college basketball followers in any sport as much as Diana Taurasi did in women's college basketball from 2000-2004? Sure you can talk about Tiger Woods in golf, Roger Federer in tennis, Derek Jeter in baseball, etc. but Taurasi really set the standard in women's college basketball and the only player who has come close to duplicating her efforts since then is Candace Parker, currently of Tennessee.

Taurasi was born in Chino, California and following a decorated high school career enrolled at the University of Connecticut before the 2000-2001 season. Her mother was adamantly against her attending UConn and going so far away from home and wanted her to stay closer to home and play at nearby UCLA. But Taurasi knew as soon as she first met Auriemma that she had a connection with him, be it from their Italian heritages, similar personalities or just her desire to play for him and knew she wanted to follow her dream and play for one of the top two programs in the country, Connecticut. Actually it was her desire right from the start to make Connecticut the top program in the country and in her career she didn't stray to far from that desire.

Taurasi did it all at UConn even as a freshman. And it all looked so simple. She had breathtaking no-look passes through traffic, pull up 25 footers and a defensive quickness that belied the fact that she was not fleet a foot.

All told in her collegiate career, Taurasi helped the Huskies to a 139-8 overall record including a remarkable 22-1 mark in the NCAA Tournament. She won three National Championships along with four Big East Conference regular season titles and two Big East Tournament crowns.

Taurasi was only the fifth two time winner of the Naismith Player of the Year Award and was awarded the Wade Trophy in 2003. She was named to the 2003 and 2004 Big East Player of the Year, and was the only then current student athlete to be selected to the Big East Silver Anniversary team. But those are only statistics. What Taurasi specifically did for her team against Tennessee was even more significant as she had the ability to make each player better.

Maria Conlon, not the most decorated player in college became one of the great college point guards during her career largely because she was playing next to Taurasi.

The legend of Taurasi in the UConn-Tennessee series all began December 30, 2000 at the Hartford Civic Center when Taurasi contributed 12 points that included a key 3 pointer with five minutes left to hold Tennessee at bay. Top ranked Connecticut held off number 2 Tennessee 81-76 in Hartford.

After the game Summitt said in a press conference attended by mostly UConn writers "is this really what I have to look forward to for the next four years." When one of the writers said "yes", Summitt just shook her head.

Three months later Tennessee got the better of the Huskies 92-88 but couldn't stop Taurasi who had 24 points in only 27 minutes of play including 6-0 from three point land.

Taurasi and the Vols next saw action in January, 2002 and Diana exploded for 32 points as UConn won by 14 at Tennessee before 24,611 fans.

Perhaps Taurasi's greatest effort in the series was in a 63-62 victory on January 4, 2003 in which she had 25 points on 9-17 shooting, 8 rebounds and 3 assists. On top of all that Taurasi hit a half court shot with time running out at the end of the first half and the time shot and regulation almost at the buzzer and the game winner with 31 seconds left in overtime. After the game Auriemma said that "we won because we were at home, had a great crowd and have the best player in the country." Summitt echoed those comments by saying "when you have a Diana Taurasi, you're never out of it."

On April 8, 2003, Taurasi led her team to one of three consecutive National Championships against Tennessee with 28 points in an upset victory. She ignored a sore back and ankle and carried the Huskies to a 73-68 victory. Fellow Husky Ann Strother said after the game "she is the most amazing leader you could ask for and she just took control."

Taurasi's career against Tennessee ended once again at the National Championship, this time on April 6, 2004. She led the Huskies to a 70-61 victory over the no. 1 Lady Vols, scoring 10 of her 17 points in the second half to help the Huskies hold off a number of charges by the Lady Vols and improve to 5-0 in the Championship game, including 4-0 against Tennessee. Tennessee had come back from a 17 point deficit in the first half to cut the score to 36-33 early in the second half but Taurasi connected on a key three point field goal and the Huskies never looked back.

She finished her career against Tennessee with a 21.6 scoring average which is the highest scoring average by any player in the history of the long and storied series.

She is currently the star for the Phoenix Mercury of the WNBA and just earned a WNBA Championship along side Rutgers star Cappie Pondexter. That journey may have been made easier recently when Phoenix acquired star Rutgers guard Cappie Pondexter.

Bird may be the most clutch player in UConn women's basketball history outside of Taurasi and she may well be the very best athlete. At least Dailey, UConn's Associate Head Coach thinks so. Bird was an equally adept basketball and soccer player at Syosset High School in New York before she transferred to basketball power Christ The King to concentrate solely on her basketball efforts.

Ross, the Mississippi coach noted that "Tennessee tried to control the paint in almost all games against UConn so they were susceptible to the smart long range bomber like Bird." And Bird made many of her threes count against the Lady Vols.

Ralph said that "we opened it up against Tennessee with our back door" and as a result of that Bird was able to hit her long range shots.

During her four year tenure at UConn the Huskies posted an unbelievable 136-9 record and won a pair of NCAA crowns in 2000 and 2002. They also advanced in 2001 Final Four, losing to Notre Dame.

Marciniak noted that "(she) has some Holdsclaw in her and some Catchings as well. She is just a phenomenal player who comes up big in all games."

Bird was the 2002 Naismith Player of the Year and Wade Trophy recipient and was named 2002 National Player of the Year by the Associated Press and the United States Basketball Writers Association. She was a three time Nancy Lieberman National Point Guard of the Year honoree and in 2002 won the ESPY as the top female college athlete of the year.

Bird had some incredible games against Tennessee, including a 25 point performance at Knoxville that single handedly led the Huskies to a 74-67 win on January 8, 2000.

Marciniak played with her for a year professionally and called her "a quiet assassin who was far more effective in games than in practices. She was a gamer, nothing more nothing less."

Holdsclaw of Tennessee is what we would characterize as the first major star in the modern era of women's college basketball. That is the era really signified by the start of the UConn and Tennessee rivalry.

Ross noted during an interview that she (Holdsclaw), "she was born to play in big games. She did not get intimidated at all and was a real gamer."

Holdsclaw grew up in Flushing, New York. She was raised by her grandmother June Elain who was a former high school basketball star in Camden, Alabama. Holdsclaw attended Christ The King high school in Queens, New York and played for Vince Cannizzaro, the same school and coach as Bird but a few years before. She became a legend not only at Christ The King but on the playgrounds of both Flushing and Queens, often times playing and beating boys, both shorter and taller than her.

At Christ The King she led her team to four straight New York State championships and then went on to Tennessee after a fierce recruiting war with teams such as UConn, North Carolina and Duke. She led the Lady Vols to three consecutive National Championships from 1996-98 and the 1998 championship was Tennessee's first ever undefeated season at 39-0.

At Tennessee she was a four time All-American and is only one of six women in the history of women's college basketball to earn that honor. She finished her career with 3,025 points and 1,295 rebounds making her the all time leading scorer and rebounder at Tennessee in either men's or women's basketball history.

In 2006, Holdsclaw was named to the women's college basketball Silver Anniversary team for being picked as one of the twenty five greatest players of all time.

Holdsclaw had a series of great games against the Huskies and was instrumental in their three straight wins from 1997-99. In the January 10, 1999 game she scored 25 points to lead Tennessee to a 92-81 road victory. At the time Tennessee was ranked no. 2 and UConn was ranked no. 1. After the game the teams swapped spots.

Semeka Randall was one of the most highly recruited players in the country in her senior year of high school coming out of Cleveland, Ohio. She is also one of the few players who narrowed her college choice down to solely UConn and Tennessee. It is an interesting phenomenon that in UConn and Tennessee, the two premier programs in the country very few players come down to both of them. Shea Ralph did and Maya Moore did this past year, both of whom are discussed along with some other players who came down to UConn and Tennessee later in this book. Randall was a trailblazer in that regard as she was one of the first players who did come down to just UConn and Tennessee. Auriemma was quite upset when she chose Tennessee and it was a very difficult conversation that she had with Auriemma on both ends. That said, she had one of the great Tennessee careers in history against UConn, a career even better than Tamika Catchings who is considered by virtually every scribe as a better player both on the collegiate and on the WNBA level even to this day.

Randall, when asked about the concept noted that "I really got up for the UConn games." This was never more obvious than in the February 2000 game at

Gampel. Randall right from the get go had a fire in her eyes that would not subside until she hit the winning floater with a few seconds left on the clock. At one juncture during the game, she landed very hard on the scorer's table but rolled right off and got back into the play without missing a beat.

Ross noted that Randall "might not have had the greatest talent in the world but she was a fierce competitor and that counted for a lot in the UConn-Tennessee series.

Randall had 25 points along with Holdsclaw in the 92-81 win on January 10, 1990 and sunk the winner with 4.4 seconds to go in a 72-71 victory over UConn at Storrs on February 2, 2000 when the Huskies were ranked no. 1 and the Lady Vols no. 4. Marciniak noted that Randall was "a fire plug. She played on pure emotion for 40 minutes. She's a player that a rivalry such as UConn-Tennessee means everything to and she took it on personally as a challenge."

Ralph noted that she guarded Randall often and was always tough to play against. She called her very athletic and "mean" but not mean in a bad way. She knew how to get under players' skins and took advantage of the little things such as grabbing a player's uniform when the referees weren't watching. It was always a great deal of shoving, pushing and elbows when they teamed up against each other in the UConn-Tennessee matches.

Randall is now an assistant basketball coach for the University of West Virginia women's team and their chief recruiter. She was formally an assistant at Michigan State along with Al Brown, former Tennessee assistant under Summit.

Shea Ralph is a North Carolina native. Her mother grew up playing college basketball with Summit and many in the know felt that she was signed, sealed and delivered to attend Tennessee by the time she was in the ninth grade. She was a frequent attendee at the University of Tennessee summer basketball camp run by Summit as was her mother Marsha.

Ralph was also torn between attending UConn and Tennessee and ultimately chose UConn after a very strong campus visit and meeting with Auriemma. Some in the know claim that Tennessee had backed off of her before her commitment but others say that Summit was shocked when she received the telephone call from Ralph indicating that she would be attending UConn.

Ralph was a staple in the UConn offensive and defensive arsenal in all the games she played against Tennessee despite her numerous injuries and perhaps had her finest game in the 2000 National Championship game in Philadelphia, a 71-52 UConn win. She was MVP of the Final Four.

Ralph played 28 minutes in the game due to foul trouble but still managed to lead her team in scoring with 15 points on 7-8 shooting from the field and had 7 assists, 6 steals, 3 rebounds and a block.

Ralph sparked UConn to a 21-6 run and she did the same in the second half with a lay up and a driving jumper to make it 36-19, a lead that Tennessee simply could not overcome.

Summitt said after the game that "Shea Ralph is the hustle player of the year on that team and gives them so much energy. She's a great leader by example."

Ralph noted that "when you are in the position that we were in this year (2000), you can't let that slip through your fingers, you never know when you're going to have it again."

Ralph was very objective about herself. She said that she was not the best athlete in the world but she knew how to play basketball and that along with little techniques on defense that she picked up along the road made her a much better player and a tough competitor in the Tennessee series.

Immediately at the end of the game Ralph tackled Bird in a friendly fashion and they dived to the floor as the Huskies celebrated in front of their ecstatic fans.

Ralph fought through 3 fouls at halftime and with her performance made her prior knee injuries and medical redshirt season a thing of the past.

Marciniak notes that Ralph probably had something to prove to Summitt in the games against UConn and her all around hustle was a perfect ingredient for a rivalry game as intense as UConn-Tennessee.

Ralph is now an assistant basketball coach at the University of Pittsburgh and it wouldn't surprise anyone if she ended up back at UConn someday as a head coach, an associates head coach or an assistant coach. She is that revered in the State of Connecticut.

The above five players represent the players who had the greatest impact on the UConn-Tennessee series during their careers.

It would obviously be remiss if we did not talk about Candace Parker of Tennessee, who may one day be the greatest player to ever play in the UConn-Tennessee series. That includes Taurasi. She is not yet, but entering this season she will only be a redshirt junior. She couldn't play her freshman year due to an ACL injury so she redshirted. Kind of unique for a superstar. She was National High School Player of the Year coming out of high school and always wanted to go to Tennessee so there was no fierce recruiting war like with other players.

This past year Parker not only had a coming out party against UConn at the Hartford Civic Center but helped Tennessee win their 7th National Championship in Cleveland. She helped them win their 8th in Tampa the following year.

In Parker's first game against UConn at home in 2006 she helped her team to a victory against UConn by scoring 13 points along with Zolman and Fluker. In that game it was obvious that Parker was an unselfish player when it came to distributing the ball and her abilities as a shooter and a shot blocker, even at 6'4" were well beyond any player in the college game.

Parker had perhaps her coming out party against UConn at the Hartford Civic Center in early 2007. UConn was ranked no. 5 entering the game and Tennessee was no. 4. Parker had a good first game against UConn the year before but was clearly looking to make her mark against UConn in the storied rivalry. Well she did in Tennessee's 70-64 win on January 6, 2007.

She scored 30 points, including the sixth dunk of her college career and grabbed 12 rebounds and blocked 6 shots to help Tennessee hold off UConn at the end.

She didn't start out real well, missing 5 of her first 6 shots but got as Summitt said "better and better" as they game went on.

Parker's dunk came with UConn well behind in double digits and seemed to ignite the Huskies who cut a big Tennessee lead to 1 but Parker took the game over down in the stretch and never let UConn take the lead by her stellar play both on the offensive and defensive ends.

With Tennessee only up 63-60 with minutes left to play Parker scored brilliantly on a driving lay up to just beat the shot clock and extend the lead to 5. Tennessee never looked back.

Auriemma marveled at Parker's play at the end of the game noting that she is one of the best one on one players he has ever seen. Was that a knock on her as a team player or just a compliment? It is tough to tell because when Auriemma says something he often is looking for a far different response. With the dunk Parker became only the fifth women's college basketball player to dunk, joining Michelle Snow of Tennessee from 2000-2002 with three dunks. No Tennessee player had ever dunked against UConn.

Parker noted after playing UConn that "we know that UConn is a great team and they're going to make our game much better and stronger during this rivalry."

The counterpunch has always been the backbone of the Connecticut-Tennessee rivalry. Connecticut wins the 1995 National Championship; Tennessee responds with the next three. UConn wins from 2002-2004, Tennessee responds in 2007. UConn gets Rebecca Lobo, Tennessee gets Chamique Holdsclaw. Then UConn gets Diana Taurasi. And now Tennessee has Candace Parker.

It had been widely assumed there would never be another Taurasi. There would never be another who could parlay outrageous talent with such chutzpah. But there is.

Parker may be the most talented player in the history of the women's college game. Not even Taurasi, hampered by her height, has the completeness of Parker's game.

And so came the UConn-Tennessee game of 2007. It was early January in Hartford. The Huskies were still searching for an identity. The Lady Vols had one: When in doubt, give it to the best player.

And what a day.

Forget that Parker tap danced on the Huskies with 30 points, 12 rebounds, six blocks and four assists in Tennessee's eventual victory. Her day wasn't just the "what" but the "when." That means when Tennessee needed a quick pick-me-up the most, Candace Parker was the ambulance driver.

First, she dunked. And it wasn't contrived. It was a within-the-flow-of-the-game hammer that was exactly the right play to make at the time. The dunk, though, was merely part of a two-minute highlight film early in the second half that had to make even the most ardent UConn women's supporter sit there and think, "Holy Memorable Moments."

The Parker portion of the program began at the 18:54 mark of the second half when she went into the lane and hit a lefty hook that would have had Dave Cowens clapping. Then teammate Sidney Spencer stole the ball and passed it to Parker on the dead run. Parker threw one down. Then she blocked a shot. Then she led the break and fed teammate Nicky Anosike a no-look pass that resulted in a layup. And then she scored 10 points in the last 10 minutes, all while the Huskies were on an all-out safety blitz, erasing an 18-point deficit. "You're going to think I'm making this up," UConn coach Auriemma said. "I said going into the game Tennessee is going to score 70 and I said I think we can get 71. If Candace gets 30, I said, 'I don't care if she gets 40, if we do a good job on the other guys.' We killed ourselves in the first half (allowing) six threes and the only one they got in the second half was a backbreaker. We take away the threes, we win the game."

Maybe, maybe not. But there was no denying that Parker was the postgame focus. One Connecticut writer called her the "Doctoress of Dunk," and suggested that Connecticut Sun coach Mike Thibault "trade his whole team, three slot machines, two craps tables and the Starbucks at the casino, just in case Parker declares herself eligible for the WNBA draft this spring. Or maybe just keep Katie Douglas and the craps tables."

Turned out Parker stayed in school. After the game, Parker discussed her dunk with all the emotion of a funeral director. "Two points is two points," she said on the podium. Parker didn't say much on the podium. When Tennessee was finished with the formal postgame news conference, several writers, understanding the significance of the dunk, sought more time with Parker. A Tennessee media relations assistant whisked Parker down the long hallway to the locker room. No more interviews. The writers were not happy. Most of them trailed Parker and yelled at the media relations assistant. The message: Proponents of the women's game shouldn't complain about the lack of media coverage if the media is more interested in coverage than the participants. Perhaps the message sunk in. Parker was made available outside the locker room for about 10 more minutes after she had showered.

Someone asked Parker if she really meant "two points is two points," given that it happened on national television, with the gallery in full throat and rising in expectation, and on The Enemy's court. "Maybe," she conceded. "But it was two points on the scoreboard."

Parker's short answers should in no way convey that she is short on personality. Just the opposite, actually. She has some of the same wiseapple that Taurasi has, only making her more endearing, and positively vital to the future of the game. Before she spoke to reporters outside the locker room, she saw ESPN.com columnist Mechelle Voepel's iPod that had a microphone attached, turning it into a recorder. "Cool!" she said, completely unsolicited. She fanned herself during the interviews, reflecting the hot shower she had just taken and the temperature inside the bowels of the Civic Center at the time. She even made Tennessee coach Pat Summitt chuckle during the game.

"I think this has been her only 40-minute game," Summitt said. "She grabbed me in the first half and said, 'Don't take your timeouts home with you, coach.' I laughed. I knew she'd have to go the distance." Summitt remembers being at home when she learned Parker would wear orange, following what Summitt called a "recruiting battle ... with negative recruiting a big part of it." "I knew if she came to Tennessee, it would be something special," Summitt said. "I've seen her do things like that (the stretch of brilliance early in the second half) and I don't take it for granted. "From the beginning of the season until now, she's playing with a lot more passion. It's important that she doesn't take possessions off. To me, she's the best player in the game." To UConn coach Geno Auriemma, too. "Cheryl Miller (USC) was big enough to do those type of things back in the day," Auriemma said. "But I think the time Candace spent with the U.S. team (in the world championships), being around them, gaining that experience, I just think her intensity level and her concentration is so much better than before. All the skills she has are more evident now. Before she'd lose some of her focus. They have the best player."

Auriemma, who has been critical of the way officials have called past Tennessee-UConn games, was amused to hear Summitt's synopsis after the game. She feels Parker doesn't get the benefitf enough whistles. "She gets fouled on about every play," Summitt said. "She plays so high up ... I don't think she gets to the line as much as she should." Auriemma retorted, "I'm sure that message has gotten to the officials. Diana shot less free throws than any great player in the history of college basketball."

> I think Candace Parker is really a dominant player. The improvement in her game is tremendous in a lot of areas. She is a player that has great composure, but I think she has a lot of different ways in which she can beat you; off the dribble, posting up. She uses her left hand, right hand. She's got the up and under, the hook shot. It's really special for us to have a player like that because she can establish the inside game unlike any other player on our team. And I will say that our team really respects how she works and what she has brought to our team. Candace is a very unselfish player and I know she is very mindful of getting her teammates the ball. Pat Summitt.

And maybe that's not the only thing Parker and Taurasi share. "It's kinda like when we had Diana," Auriemma said. "What's the answer (to stopping her)? There is no answer, sometimes." Parker stayed in school, allowing her body to rest. She played in the fall of 2006 for Thibault and Seattle Storm coach Anne Donovan at the World Championships in Brazil. She played the entire college season. She finally had a chance to rest. But the season she had, culminating with the national championship, had coaches across the country saluting. "When coaches prepare and scout Candace Parker, no one's thinking about the 'Candace Revolution' or her impact on the game or what her legacy will be," Mississippi coach Carol Ross told USA Today. "We're just thinking about our game and how the heck we're going to guard her. Posts can't defend her on the perimeter, and guards can't defend her in the paint.

"She's the toughest matchup in the game. On many nights, she's the best guard on the floor, the best post on the floor, the best rebounder on the floor, the best passer on the floor and, let's not forget, the best scorer on the floor. She's got the strut of a competitor and the stuff of a champion." "Her basketball IQ is pretty high," Thibault said at the Sun's Media Day in April. She studies the game. She listens. One of the things that was fun about being around her is that besides listening, she asks questions. She wants to learn more. I enjoyed being around her." Her footprint on the college game has been fascinating. It's almost as though all of her other skills are dwarfed by the dunks. A writer asked Auriemma after the game in January if the dunk was "appropriate."

Sometimes, women's basketball writers feel a need to protect the "purity" of the game. "Hell, yeah, man, it was appropriate," Auriemma said. "I wish one of my guys would have done it. It wasn't like one of those contrived dunks like they got for Michelle Snow." She has six career dunks, the most by a women's college player, including four in five tries this season.

Clearly, Parker comes from a family of high achievers. Her dad played at Iowa. Her brother, Anthony, played at Bradley and then was a first-round draft choice of the Toronto Raptors. Her brother, Marcus, is a is a resident radiologist at Johns Hopkins. Parker ended the season as a second-team academic All-American, with a 3.29 grade point average as a sports management major. She was on course to graduate in December, 2007.

Parker was born in 1986 in St. Louis and has played not only the forward spot but also center and guard both in high school and college. She is engaged to NBA player and former Duke star, Shelden Williams currently of the Atlanta Hawks.

Parker is known for not only her game on the court but off the court. People magazine recently tabbed her as one of the 100 Most Beautiful People in the World and has a future not only as a model but as a basketball player.

Parker had the opportunity to leave school last year after December because she will be graduating. She could have entered the WNBA draft but decided to play for at least one more National Championship for Tennessee. She won that Championship.

> She is on her way. She needed the Championship last year. It is like a gymnast who needs a Gold. She can play all five positions in the pros. It depends on which team takes her. She is in the mix for greatest of all time. It is still early. She may win a couple of more Championships. *Mel Greenberg.*

Colleen Healy grew up as a small kid in the small town of Willimantic, Connecticut. She was a tomboy as a kid and had athletic skills but certainly not the skills that would have put her on the map as a star basketball player impacting a future NCAA Tournament.

Healy was a more than adequate softball and basketball player as a kid and graduated from Windham High School, receiving an athletic scholarship to the University of New Haven, a Division II school to play both softball and basketball. After a semester she knew it was the wrong place for her and she quit school. She drove home in the middle of a snow storm and her car died on the highway. That was the good news. Her father was less than happy with her decision especially since she had not consulted with him.

They talked through the night and finally they agreed that Healy would stay in college and transfer to Eastern Connecticut State University to play softball.

The next day she registered at Eastern and helped lead her team to a Division III National Championship. She didn't play basketball at Eastern Connecticut but she did practice in the gym as much as she could. At the end of the semester she told her father that she once again wanted to transfer, this time to UConn to play Division I basketball. He looked at her like she was crazy but knew well enough that if Colleen was going to follow a dream he was not going to try to stop her.

She was accepted at UConn and reenrolled there and had no chance to make the basketball team. She became the team manager and then the next year a walk on, playing with players such as Lobo. She spent that next summer practicing basketball every waking hour and in the Fall was riding an exercise bicycle when Auriemma approached her and told her that he had some good news for her. She had no idea what he was about to tell her but he ultimately told her that she had earned a basketball scholarship at UConn through her hard work and team spirit.

Healy played in a few games for UConn, usually during mop up time and actually helped her team win a regular season game on the road at Georgetown after Rizzotti fouled out and gave her a quick pep talk before she went in as the point guard replacing Rizzotti.

Healy was exhilarated by the opportunity to play against Georgetown. She had waited for that opportunity for many years and certainly didn't make the least of it. She was not nervous and played with a characteristic cool.

> *Jen was welled up in the eyes and said "Coll, you are the best ball handler on this team. Go in there and win this for me." I'll have to admit, I thought she was nuts because, clearly, she was the best ball handler. However, she and I were very close and it was quite inspirational. The next play Georgetown was taking the ball out from the sideline. I had stepped off the point guard to the degree that she felt I was not going to defend the inbound pass. Just as the ball was coming in, I sprinted toward the Georgetown point guard. She was taken off guard, caught the ball and traveled."*

Since graduation Healy has become one of the top salespeople and inspirational speakers at Merck and has broadcasted UConn women's games including games against Tennessee. Her experience was nothing like the experience of any of the aforesaid players and her statistics don't resonate in any UConn-Tennessee record book. But Healy proved over her career that she belonged in the annals of UConn basketball as much as Bird, Taurasi or Ralph. Even Auriemma wouldn't and couldn't doubt that.

We mean no offense to players like Carla Berube, Kara Wolters, Ann Strother, Kara Lawson, etc. but the aforesaid players really have stood out during their careers against the other foe and have set a standard that has rarely been duplicated at any school.

THE ASSISTANTS

Holly Warlick, Chris Dailey and Micki DeMoss. Put them in any order or jumble them up in a hat but when their names are ultimately mentioned it is impossible not to recognize their huge roles in building not only the UConn-Tennessee series but the UConn-Tennessee Programs. All are former assistant head coaches who became associate head coaches under their mentors, Auriemma and Summitt.

Let's start with Warlick. She was a backcourt whiz at Tennessee as a player who joined the basketball squad as a walk on, but also as a scholarship track athlete.

It wasn't long before she earned a basketball scholarship at Tennessee and she ultimately became the first player in the history of the University of Tennessee athletics (men or women) to have her jersey retired, which happened at the end of her career in 1980.

Warlick helped the Lady Vols reach the Final Four three times in her four years and earned Kodak All-American honors as a senior. She was also a member of the 1980 U.S. Olympic Team and played professionally with the Nebraska Wranglers in the women's professional basketball league.

Warlick just finished her 22nd season under Summitt and going into this past season had been at her side either as a player or as an assistant for 764 of her amazing 913 wins.

In June of 2001 the Women's Basketball Hall of Fame in Knoxville selected her as one of ten inductees enshrined into the Hall. Not bad for an assistant.

Warlick is not only a master tactician but also a premier recruiter. Players such as Marciniak, Catchings, and Lawson cite her along with DeMoss as primary reasons why they attended Tennessee.

Her expertise and major contributions come from her work with the guards, not only tutoring them but recruiting them. Lawson has credited her with strengthening her game as has Shanna Zolman, a three-time all-SEC selection. Zolman is one of the great three point shooters in Tennessee history and she attributes much of that to her work with Warlick.

Warlick is thrilled to be at Tennessee and has rarely if ever been mentioned for any head coaching jobs. That is her choice and not the choice of other schools. Many consider her to be an heir apparent to Summitt when and if she retires. Warlick feels that the Tennessee tradition has established "a winning way of thinking, practicing and competing." She finds the most rewarding part of her job to "watch each player grow up and mature throughout her career, both on and off the court." The Tennessee fan support to her is mind boggling.

> "Our fan support throughout the years has been insane. From the very young to the elderly, they have followed us around the world. They are very loyal to our team."

DeMoss is widely recognized as one of the greatest recruiters in the history of men's or women's college basketball.

Talk to Holdsclaw, Randall, Catchings, etc. and right after the name Summitt comes the name DeMoss as one of the reasons why this trio and others ended up in Knoxville.

DeMoss' career began at Louisiana Tech where she started and starred at point guard for her final three years.

In 1985, DeMoss was hired by Summitt to be her top assistant at Tennessee. During her 18 seasons in Knoxville the Lady Vols went to 13 Final Fours and won 6 National Championships. Throughout her tenure at Tennessee she called Summitt both a friend and a mentor. She turned down numerous opportunities to become a head coach to stay at Tennessee but when an opportunity opened at Kentucky in 2003 she couldn't turn down the fellow SEC school.

DeMoss spent four seasons at Kentucky and compiled a 71-56 record including a mark of 20-14 this past season.

It became obvious during her tenure that DeMoss preferred the x's and o's in recruiting more than she did the alumni work, the fundraising and the other duties and responsibilities attendant to being a head coach. She marveled throughout her career at Tennessee how Summitt was able to do everything she did in an almost seamless fashion. For DeMoss at Kentucky it was clearly too much.

She stated at her April 11, 2007 press conference that "this was a very difficult decision for me. After thirty years of coaching, I just wanted to step back and reassess what I want to do for the rest of my life."

DeMoss is currently the assistant coach at Texas under coach Goestenkors.

There's no denying that Geno Auriemma is the face of the UConn women's phenomenon. But if you call him the patriarch, the matriarch is Chris Dailey, the associate head coach and heartbeat of the program.

"CD," as she's known, was the captain of the women's team at Rutgers that won the last AIAW National Championship against Texas in the Palestra in 1982. She was clearly the leader of that team although she did not start. She, like Auriemma, came to Connecticut on a prayer in the mid 80s to a place with one office, one phone and absolutely no chance of ever winning a national championship.

And yet they've won five.

Dailey, both engaging and particular, has been there for the players and Auriemma every single day. Maybe the best place to start with her is to get The Questions out of the way first. The two questions she hears most are:

Why aren't you married?

Why aren't you a head coach by now?

The answer to question one: "In any relationship, you have to figure out what you're willing to live with and what you're willing to live without," she told the New London Day once. "It's probably why I'm not married. You can't change everything about a person."

The answer to question two: "When I came here after two years (as an assistant) at Rutgers, I said to myself, 'I can be a coach,'" Dailey told The Day. "I needed the challenge of building the program from the bottom. Now, I know too much. I'm not willing to go to a place that doesn't have certain things.

"If I had just come in the middle and jumped into all this, I'd be out of here," she said. "But this has been a shared venture for Geno and I. I'm fortunate to work with someone who gave me shared ownership. Part of this is mine. Sure, I have an ego, but I don't think I need to run out and get a job.

"I was flattered by Rutgers," she said, alluding to a job offer in the mid 90s. "But I hadn't been back in 10 years and it was a new experience. I make a lot of decisions based on gut instinct. A lot of times, we don't write a thing down about a kid, but we know we need her for our program. My instincts tell me Connecticut is where I need to be."

Dailey is one of the great detail people in the game. There was one classic scene after a game at West Virginia many years ago best illustrating that. Auriemma was entertaining the media well after the game ended when Dailey approached him with a look that suggested the apocalypse was close.

"Where are we going to eat? Where are we going to eat?" she asked.

Auriemma couldn't have been less interested.

"I want to go to Wendy's," Dailey said, "but the kids want TCBY. We always give in to the yogurt people."

That's how Dailey knows the players. She knows every detail about them. She knows the yogurt people.

"This is a very happy team," program alum Paige Sauer once said, "and CD is one of the big reasons. She's the one who worries about all the little things coach doesn't have time for. She takes care of everything."

With Auriemma's blessing.

"Geno is always referring to himself as the "Idea Man,'" Dailey said. "I have ideas, too, but he sees things and doesn't always know how to get things done. Because he gives me a lot of responsibility, I'm able to get things done without asking him."

Dailey has also proven to be the program's best pinch-hitter. Whenever Auriemma has been unable to coach, through administrative circumstances, family circumstances or referee circumstances, Dailey has been there to come through in the clutch.

Maybe the most memorable time came in 1997, when Auriemma missed the Big East Tournament. He was home in Pennsylvania at his father Donato's funeral. The games had to go on. UConn was undefeated at the time.

This wasn't like the first time Dailey had to coach the Huskies. That was in 1989 when she coached three games of the Big East Tournament. Auriemma had to serve a Big East suspension for inadvertently scheduling an extra game.

The first game was against Villanova, which the Huskies won easily. Auriemma's traditional seat at the end of the bench was empty. Villanova coach Harry Perretta, who unloaded one of the great coaching lines ever from a visiting coach, didn't see much of a different with Dailey at the helm:

"You ever see the movie 'Patton,' when Patton won some battle and somebody said, 'Well, Rommel's back in Germany?'" Perretta said. "But it was still Rommel's plan. You know what I mean? The plan they had is the plan they have all the time. The philosophies are the same."

Carla Berube told reporters, "It's the same system. And their styles are a lot alike. Maybe she's not as intense."

Auriemma later said he listened to the game from home. That was good, because at least somebody was listening to something. As Dailey said, "I was sweating. It was hot as heck. But it was good. The players really responded. Although now I know what Geno's talking about when he says they never listen to him."

Dailey proved to be a media/coaching star later in the tournament, leading the Huskies to the championship over Notre Dame. She was as effective coaching the team as she was entertaining the media after the game.

Hartford Courant columnist Jeff Jacobs wrote, "The first night against Villanova, she admits to perspiring. Somebody like Utah coach Rick Majerus or Patriots coach Bill Parcells would brag about sweating bullets.

But C.D.? This is an anatomical tidbit she'd rather not share unless she were under the fiercest of klieg lights with Barbara Walters. Sweat? Chris Dailey says she doesn't even perspire working out.

As long as we're on the subject of Bah-bah Wah-wah. What kind of tree is Chris Dailey? Absolutely a long, wispy willow that can bend with the emotional torrents of the guy she has shared a bench with for a dozen years."

In those days, the UConn women's fandom was still growing and still a bit wide-eyed. Every time Berube scored a basket, they would serenade her with a "Beruuuuuuube" chant that echoed throughout Gampel Pavilion. They loved Kara Wolters and Nykesha Sales and had a burgeoning love affair with Shea Ralph. But in this Big East Tournament, Dailey got the loudest applause. The program had already rewritten itself, going from national champion in 1995 to a return trip to the Final Four in 1996 to an undefeated 1997. But there was something even more special about this, the way the players rallied around Dailey.

At the end of the Notre Dame game, they lifted her on their shoulders. One state columnist wrote that it was fitting "because of the number of times CD has carried them."

This was the three days that the media and fans saw a side to Dailey they hadn't seen enough. They knew she could recruit. They knew she could relate to people of all ages. They knew she taught the players all the little things off the court of which people take note, like making sure they say "please" and "thank you."

But these were the three days that Dailey showed she can coach. She knows the game. She is as responsible as anybody else for the growth and maturation of the great post players they've had in the program.

Dailey had a chance at Rutgers. She spoke to people at Boston College. But she remained at Connecticut.

The night the Huskies beat Notre Dame, Dailey wore a red outfit. Writers joked that she must have worn the same thing to the Rutgers interview.

"I'd like to inform you this is tomato red and not Scarlet Knights of the Raritan red," she said. "Besides, I wore black and white to the interview—also Rutgers colors—and didn't get the job."

Dailey's next coaching stint came during the Huskies' second National Championship season. The first game in Hartford was the Coaches vs. Cancer challenge.

It became the "Coach" vs. Cancer Challenge midway through the first half. Auriemma's second technical foul protesting the same call earned him his first ejection since 1992, leaving the Huskies in Dailey's hands.

What Dailey and 15,777 fans then watched at the Hartford Civic Center was one of the most stirring regular season wins in a while, keeping Dailey's perfect head coaching record ... perfect.

Dailey had pinch-coached for the coach seven other times. She went to 8-0 Wednesday after UConn's 68-62 victory over Kentucky.

"Obviously, we were all a little surprised," Ralph said at the time. "We realized what (Auriemma) was doing. It's about us responding. We never respond to his challenges. He made it evident that we had to do this ourselves. He doesn't play. Last year, we got challenged and lost every big game we played in."

Maybe not every big game—but most. So without their coach, the Huskies went on a 9-0 run in the final two minutes to snap a 59-59 tie.

Ralph gave the Huskies the lead for good, 61-59, with 1 minute, 31 seconds remaining. Svetlana Abrosimova followed with the dagger—a 3-pointer with a minute left—before Ralph and Abrosimova made four straight free throws.

"It felt like we won the national championship," Ralph said. "We haven't felt that way after a game in a long, long time. Coach asked us what the difference was. We accomplished something together when we were challenged. For once, we stepped up."

Auriemma's beef with official Scott Yarborough began long before he was tossed with 5:45 left in the first half. The call in question was a hand check whistled against Kennitra Johnson, maybe 35 feet from the basket. Auriemma was hit with the technical, Kentucky's Tiffany Wait made two free throws, and before the ball was inbounded again, Auriemma drew the second—and a trip to the locker room.

"You ask the players to keep their composure and execute under adversity," Auriemma said, "and I didn't set a good example, did I?"

"My first thought was that I wanted to kill him," Dailey said. "Everyone was so emotional and I think we were able to live off that a little bit. After the emotion ran off, we just coached. Tonya (Cardoza) and Jamelle (Elliot) (the other assistant coaches) did a great job.

"I feel great for the kids," Dailey said. "We fought back, and that's a good sign for this group. Like Shea said, 'we got punched and we punched back.'"

Auriemma hadn't been tossed since Dec. 29, 1992 during a regular-season game at Vanderbilt.

"This game showed we can play with one of the top teams and that we are one of the top teams," Kentucky coach Bernadette Mattox said.

Three seasons later, Mattox became part of Connecticut basketball, joining Mike Thibault's staff with the Connecticut Sun.

A few seasons later, Chris mourned the death of her father, Bob. It was a cold, winter morning in New Brunswick, N.J. at St. John The Baptist Church. The whole team was there.

Mike DiMauro, a columnist for the New London Day, wrote the following:

"It was the mission of the man who identified himself as Father Tom to encapsulate Bob Dailey's life into a few words Tuesday morning in glacial New Brunswick, N.J., where the warmth inside St. John The Baptist Church was of both symbolic and meteorological comfort.

But what's to say about the man who had everything?

Father Tom's remembrances, though quite engaging, would have required no words, because "everything" to Bob Dailey happened to be sitting a few feet away. Indeed, Father Tom could have stood before the church and merely pointed to those first few pews, where all Bob Dailey worked for, stood for, cared about and believed in sat pensively in his honor.

Bob Dailey's daughter, familiar to the sports fans of Connecticut, sat in the front row, maybe 20 feet from Father Tom. Chris Dailey, the embodiment of everything UConn women's basketball has come to mean, joined a church full of family and friends Tuesday at her dad's funeral.

Chris Dailey sat two rows in front of the UConn women's players and coaches. The women of Storrs were there to support the woman who has always supported them. The most visible women's athletic program in the country, en masse, inside the quaint church where "CD" went to Sunday mass ... a most impressive and inspiring sight, to be sure.

Bob Dailey's illness worsened in his final days, yet the presence of his families—the Daileys and the Huskies—made them pass with less pain.

Father Tom said, "There is more to life than what we see and feel every day," reminding us that 12-room houses and Beamers are nice ... but a good life lived, a life with values and principles, will be rewarded, living on through those you've touched, long after the Beamers hit the junk yard.

You needn't have met Bob Dailey to have known him. If you've ever watched the UConn women, on—and especially off—the court, you could have written the biography.

The values Bob Dailey instilled in his daughter are the same ones his daughter cultivates in the women of Storrs. The UConn women are everything in which Chris Dailey and Geno Auriemma believe, because Chris Dailey and Geno Auriemma come from everything in which their parents, Donato and Marsiella Auriemma, and Bob and Mary Dailey, have believed.

Chris Dailey's role in building this program to the moon and back began with rolled-up sleeves, mixing the cement with the Italian guy. The evolution of Dailey's niche has been unlike what befalls every other associate head basketball coach in the country.

Dailey is one of the most recognizable figures in the State of Connecticut and that includes politicians, industry leaders and athletes. She has been at Auriemma's side at UConn ever since he took over the helm in 1985.

Chris Dailey, willingly and appreciatively, is everything from stand-in mother to the players while they are on campus, to educator, confidante, moral compass ... and lest we all forget she can teach a post move or two to players such as Kara Wolters.

Dailey is also a premier recruiter and has been instrumental in coaxing many a UConn recruit to play for the Huskies. Ralph noted that she had been recruited at Tennessee directly by Summitt and at UConn mostly by Dailey and not Auriemma. She was very much attracted to Dailey's understated but firm recruiting techniques and she cites Dailey as one of her many reasons why she ended up as a Husky as opposed to a Lady Vol.

She has been daughter and coach that particular season, making frequent drives home to be with her father. Bob Dailey's last days came watching the UConn women approach the women's NCAA record for most consecutive wins. While the players (hell, the whole state) celebrated the extraordinary overtime win over Tennessee earlier this month, Chris drove home that night to spend more time with him.

The UConn women's fandom is often mocked for its breathlessness—but mostly for the advanced ages of its constituents. Mr. Dailey was part of Husky Nation for many years, but in his final days, the UConn women comforted him as only his family could.

It's here you wonder just how many people of our state believe in the UConn women because they're the most reliable compartment in their lives. Sure, their fans' health might be failing, old age might be daunting, getting around is a pain in the you-know-where ... but the girls are on TV tonight, and so that means it's a good day.

And if they can get tickets to a game? It might help more than the medicine.

It's doubtful Chris Dailey knew the tentacles this program would grow when she worked with Auriemma from a tiny office, one telephone and all, 18 years ago. Yet for the last few months, the Huskies were a constant, a diversion and a winner for her dad, comforting Bob Dailey the way they have so many in this state.

Maybe it's the least they could do for Mr. Dailey, whose good life lived provided his daughter the values she's imparted to mold this remarkable program into the beacon it has become.

Father Tom related an anecdote or two about Bob Dailey's fishing exploits, devotion to his family, and love of the UConn women.

And through it all, the women of Storrs hung on every word, learning of a man and his values, the ones they'll use wherever life takes them.

Bob Dailey lives on, indeed.

LIFE AFTER UCONN AND TENNESSEE

Many UConn and Tennessee players ultimately play in the WNBA. It is the nature of the beast and the fact that the most talented players are at UConn and Tennessee. Mel Greenberg, noted women's commentator has said that "if you want to play in the WNBA then go to Tennessee and if you want to win national championships then go to UConn." In reality, more WNBA players have come from UConn than from Tennessee. Two players, Nykesha Sales and Asjha Jones have grown tremendously as people, personalities and players in the WNBA and have thrived in the process. They were both relatively quiet in college off the court, but certainly thrived in college on the court winning multiple National Championships.

Sales has one of the most famous, or perhaps infamous, names in women's basketball.

Jones, with immense talent, is far more anonymous and has been such ever since entering UConn with one of the most famous recruiting classes in history which included Sue Bird, Swin Cash and Tamika Williams.

But those who have known Sales and Jones for the duration of their college and adult careers also know they could be the test cases for the value of playing college basketball at UConn or Tennessee for that matter. The programs, because of the spotlights they command, prepare their players better for the WNBA and in many instances, for life in general.

Begin with Sales. Aside from being an all-time player, she was part of an all-time incident, a staged basket at Villanova once night in 1997 that earned her the UConn career scoring title—and Geno Auriemma headlines across the country for "compromising the integrity of the game."

Cool Keesh, as she's called, has become quite the young woman, miles and miles from her days as a shy kid from Bloomfield. Conn., about 20 minutes from Hartford.

There was no siren, no honk-honk of the horn and no flashing lights when Sales arrived as a basketball player. It was done on her time at her pace, because NST (Nykesha Standard Time) is nothing, if not, well, definitely approximate. That is who she is.

Yet to see her playing in the WNBA with the Connecticut Sun, is to see a player who has become comfortable with herself. The girl they've always known in Connecticut is all grown up now, a young woman. She is no longer the shy high school kid from Bloomfield High School in Connecticut who entered the University of Connecticut along with one of the greatest recruiting classes in the history of men's or women's college basketball.

"People say I've changed," Sales told the New London Day once. "I guess I have. I mean, I'm one of the oldest on the team now. There are certain things that come with that."

It is impossible to appreciate the woman Sales has become without understanding the kid she used to be. Growing up, there was Nykesha, parents Kim and Ray and brother Brooks. There was the home on Pasture Lane in Bloomfield.

"It was my family, my brother, maybe seven or eight friends," Sales said. "We called it 'our little crew.' And then, just like that, everyone was splitting up."

Sales' final two college choices were UConn and Ohio State. Auriemma had a feeling Sales' closeness to her family would ultimately send her to Storrs. But one fall Saturday in 1993 didn't hurt the cause.

Part of Sales' recruiting trip to Ohio State featured a Saturday football game at Ohio Stadium, "the Big Horseshoe," part of college football lore and legend. One problem: It snowed. A reporter friend called Auriemma at his home and told him to turn on the TV.

"Yessssssss!" Auriemma yelled in his best Marv Albert voice, knowing Sales' aversion to snow. And off to UConn she went, an infinitely talented, scared young woman. "Pam Webber," Sales replied without hesitation, when asked the biggest influence on her in the early years at Storrs. "She was my roommate on the road.

She was really good to me. Because I got to know Pam, it was easy to know Rebecca (Lobo). Plus, Jamelle (Elliot) was my recruiting host."

The person Sales has become is tied to her experiences in college at UConn. She was forced to meet different people than she ever grew up with and interact with adults and media members.

"It's a lot easier for me now talking to people. I don't even think about it," Sales told The Day. "I'm not ghetto or anything. What I mean by that is I can shake someone's hand and say, 'Hi, how are you?' and not 's'up' and keep rollin.' I've matured in that sense. When this all started, I didn't say much. I've opened up more. But if I'm still stand-offish, you're not there yet."

Sales had a successful, and colorful college career, beginning with the nickname her teammates gave her.

"How did 'Precious?' begin?"

"How did you know about that?" she asks.

"Precious" is the nickname UConn teammates gave to Sales because Auriemma never yelled at her. Of course, it was mostly "Keesh" or "Kesha" unless they wanted to bust a few chops. Rita Williams is the likely source for "Precious," when she wasn't calling her friend, "MJ."

"(Auriemma) even yelled at coach (Chris) Dailey," Sales grinned, "but not me. He never could." Auriemma might tell you that Sales is his all-time favorite UConn player, despite the ignominious event that will link him and Sales, for the foreseeable future. Sales is also one of his top five players of all-time.

Auriemma knew Sales was the most talented player he'd ever coached, pre-Taurasi. He also knew she was the most selfless, consistently deferring to teammates who didn't have her skills. One of the reasons the 1996-97 team was 33-0 before the regional final loss to Tennessee was because Sales, the preseason Player of the Year, often deferred to Kara Wolters. Sales has always been big on deference.

And that was the fuel behind The Layup. Auriemma knew Sales could have had the school scoring record easily, had she not been afflicted with unselfishness. The layup Auriemma staged in Feb. 1997 to get Sales the two points she needed to break Kerry Bascom's school record—after Sales snapped her Achilles' tendon one point short—was repayment for her selflessness. It became national news.

"I would go places and I'd hear, 'there's the girl who made the shot,'" Sales said. "We went to a taping of the Cosby show and the comedian who comes out before the show starts found out I was there. When Bill Cosby came out, the comedian said, 'Bill, do you know Nykesha Sales?' And he started limping."

Auriemma was accused of corrupting the integrity of the game. He feuded with the media. It wasn't Nykesha Sales, it was Soupy Sales, wrote Hartford Courant sports columnist Jeff Jacobs, who was bombarded with angry letters.

When asked what her reaction to "Soupy Sales" was seven years ago, Sales replied, "Who?" Believe it or not, I really didn't read a lot of the articles about it. I was in the hospital because I had surgery (to her Achilles). I didn't see what was written, but I know some of those poor reporters got it pretty good."

Sales' maturity with the Sun has become through a great relationship with coach Mike Thibault, who allows his players significant input into the franchise's decision-making. After their first year of getting to know each other, Thibault noticed Sales' willingness to express an opinion.

"She started asking me who we were going to draft," Thibault told The Day. "She even called me and said, 'Coach, this (Lindsay) Whalen kid is really good.'"

Sales, innocently aloof at times, had never shown Thibault the interest in roster moves. "No, I didn't get the impression she had been (interested)," Thibault said. "Championship teams don't happen without the best players being the hardest workers. Keesh has been more consistent with her leadership qualities. More vocal. More outgoing."

One night during a Sun game, while the players are asked questions about themselves that are recorded and played on the arena video board, one of the topics was which candy the players preferred, Starburst or Skittles. Sales often masks her emotions from the public, but in this instance, she played for laughs. "Skittles," she deadpanned. "Starburst are a pain in the neck to open.

"It was just me and the (cameraman) chitchatting, sort of being silly with the questions, so that's the jump-off I came with," Sales said. "I'm up and down. I'm not saying that's good or bad. Sometimes I need my space and sometimes I'm in the mix. I don't shut down, but I'm quiet. It might seem like I'm shy or whatever you want to call it."

Thibault told The Day, "Part of maturity is growing up. To know who you are. To be comfortable with who you are. I don't think she goes around every day feeling that she has to prove herself to somebody. She knows what she's capable of on the court and she knows who she is as a person. She's growing up."

On the floor, Sales has become, as in college an underappreciated player … who still manages to make the all-star team. In 2005, she was having an MVP-type season, even if she knew she had no chance to win it. The year before, Sales had a chance to win the WNBA title for the Sun. She dropped 30 on Seattle in what could have been the deciding game. With the Sun down two in the final seconds, Sales missed a 3-point shot that would have won the Sun their first title.

It was the kind of play that could define a career. And create a miserable offseason. Maybe a carryover into the next season.

"Shoot," Thibault told reporters in response, "I don't think Keesh thinks about the shot she took 10 minutes ago. That's what makes a great player."

She didn't win the MVP, as one writer suggested, because of the "WNBA caste system. "Once you are branded a Toyota Camry—steady, reliable—there's no chance of becoming a Beamer."

In 2005, Sales joined Sheryl Swoopes as the only two players in the history of the league with 3,000 points, 500 steals and 400 assists. But that's where the comparisons with Swoopes end. Their numbers are similar, but the perceptions aren't.

Sales had a difficult 2006 season, battling Achilles' and hip injuries. During one game, Sheri Sam, a contemporary of Sales,' made her way to the basket for a yawningly easy layup with Sales guarding her. After Sam tied the game, Thibault removed Sales from the game for the final time. She sat out the next month.

"I'm just not able to do the things I'm used to doing," Sales said after that game. "My legs just aren't there. I probably should have sat a long time ago, but we're in a crucial part of the season I should have done it a long time ago, to be honest. I'm digging a hole. Not just my body, but mentally, it's getting worse. It's like I just see a white cloud out there. I've never been in this position before."

Sales has been quite lucky to play in 248 straight games. She spent the off season of 2006 healing and making public appearances near Mohegan Sun, where the Sun play their home games. Public appearances for Sales? It would have been unheard of in college. She was simply too shy. That has all changed.

Sales was hanging out with 20 little kids at the Build-A-Bear store inside Crystal Mall in Waterford. There was Cool Keesh stuffing her bear and then dressing it in a Connecticut Sun uniform, fitting right in with all the little kids whose excitement level indicated that either Christmas was coming soon or they all ate their own bag of M&M's just before arrival.

Sales looked great and sounded better, even though she hadn't picked up a basketball in earnest since the Sun's exit from the 2006 playoffs. The 2006 season gave Sales a nudge toward mortality. Sore hip, tender Achilles, a month missed and even a tenuous place back in the lineup, stuck in the middle of a team that caught fire without her.

"I really didn't know what to think," Sales said between Build-A-Bear moments. "When I came back, the pain was tolerable, but I wasn't my normal self. I'd never missed that many games. If I came back and tried to do my normal thing ... what if the outcome of the games weren't the same?

"Everyone was great," Sales said. "KT (Katie Douglas) told me to keep shooting. Coach T (Thibault) told me to keep shooting. But I didn't feel like I had a rhythm."

"Once I get back to training, I'll be fine," Sales said. "I was in an unfamiliar place last year. Even though you still have it, sometimes it's hard to find. A lot goes into this that people don't realize. Mental, physical ... there are a lot of parts."

Sales knows that most, if not all, of her teammates from the 1995 national championship team at UConn have succumbed to basketball mortality. Rebecca Lobo is a mother and sports commentator. Jennifer Rizzotti is a mother and a coach. Kim Better is pregnant. Carla Berube is a coach.

And yet Sales is still a player, a good one, a player the Sun needed badly in 2007.

"Right now, I just feel like I need more time to prepare than I did before," Sales said. "I know I have to stretch a little more, get more treatment, pay more attention."

All the ailments, Sales admitted, nag at her, as they always will. But Sales, who will turn 31 on May 10, feels like a Toyota with 100,000 miles on it: It's not new, but not nearly done.

Her destination after Build-A-Bear was Storrs, where she'd work out with the UConn women, the first time she'd run up and down the floor since late August. UConn coach Geno Auriemma loves it when Sales returns to practice, if for no other reason than they can't guard her and he has reason to bark.

Cool Keesh looked and sounded exactly as every Sun fan would have hoped earlier this week. There's some gas left in the tank. More than enough for at least another five years in the WNBA.

Jones, meanwhile, has found a home in Connecticut with the Sun, following he college home in Connecticut with the Huskies. Her career has skyrocketed.

Jones is a powerful 6'2" forward with great offensive skills and a mid-range jumper that at times appears to be unstoppable.

She grew up in Piscataway, New Jersey and was the subject of a great recruiting war between UConn and Rutgers which is right down the road. UConn ultimately won because she wanted to get away from home and play for Coach Auriemma.

"Man, I love winning," Jones says.

She didn't do much of it at her first WNBA stop in Washington. They won nine games in 2003. Her team in Connecticut won its ninth game before half the 2004 season ended.

"Nine wins all season ... I came from UConn where we lost nine games in four years. To win only nine in a season is really difficult," she said.

But then, Jones had grown used to "difficult," especially after the 9-25 record in Washington and an off-season experience in Russia. She experienced an acclaimed Russian winter, presumably without a babushka to keep her face warm or sufficient vodka (to keep everything else warm). And one other thing.

"They're not accustomed to seeing people who look like me," Jones said diplomatically, noting that 6-foot-2 African-American women aren't exactly as common there as borscht.

Jones had been playing overseas not long after buying a townhouse in Maryland, only to discover the Mystics traded her a few days later.

"Isn't that the curse?" she said. "Someone buys a house and they get traded. I haven't even stayed there yet. When I bought it, I went to Italy for three days then I got traded. All of my (stuff) is still in there."

Jones cited her UConn experience—extensive travel, meeting many different kinds of people—that has helped her on and off the court.

"For us right now, it's more the way it was (at UConn)," Jones said. "No one gets 30 and no one gets five.... (At Washington), I got my shots when I played, but not everyone did. That's not the winning edge. If you play that way and win, fine. But if you're not winning and that stuff goes on, it looks really bad."

And that's why it feels really good for Jones right now.

"I'm in the place I want to be right now," Jones said. "I'm having a good time."

Auriemma was on record several times as saying Jones was the most talented member of the Cash/Bird/Williams/Jones recruiting class—and that it was entirely up to her when she wanted to prove it to everyone. There was, however, never any doubting her character. On Senior Night, 2002, Auriemma was asked to describe Jones and said, "You know when you drive up to an estate and you see a huge marble pillar? It sets the tone for what's inside. That's Asjha."

The transition has been easy with Thibault.

"It's easy to play for him," Jones said. "There's no such thing as a bad shot, as long as you're balanced. He won't ream you out. He doesn't make you feel pressured, yet in a way, he guides you to what needs to be done.

"He's my personal passer during pregame (shooting drills)," Jones said. "Any coach who is that hands on, you want to play hard for him. I wouldn't have gone just anywhere. I think the only place I'd have come is right here."

There's no denying that Jones, Bird, Cash and Williams have enjoyed successful WNBA careers. Jones, a starter for the 2007 season with the Sun, might have the brightest future.

"There are moments," Jones said during a 2006 interview with The Day. "But I'm definitely not there yet. You know how some nights you feel pretty good and some nights you're just OK and you get through it?"

Asked if she's surpassed Bird, Williams and Cash, Jones said, "Are you trying to set me up? I have no idea. I don't read papers and I don't know what's really going on. I know Tamika is getting her legs back (from off season knee injury), Swin is still working back (from a knee injury late in the 2004 season) and Sue is so far away (in Seattle).

"Coach Auriemma always said that eventually, I'll get it," Jones said. "I always have to plan things out in my head." She now gets it.

Life has been a little different for both Bird and Taurasi. They play respectively in the WNBA for Seattle and Phoenix and have had similar experiences to both Jones and Sales. One big difference is that they also play in Russia in the off season and it has been to say the least a serious maturation process.

They are both treated like royalty in Russia both from a financial perspective and in terms of their living arrangements. Taurasi earns almost ten times her annual salary in the WNBA and Bird earns almost three times her WNBA salary in Russia. They play there from December to mid May and live in a rent free, six bedroom villa that is quite lavish. It includes an indoor swimming pool and a sauna. They both have a part time cook and an interpreter along with personal drivers. They receive a stipend for flights back to the United States. Certainly not a WNBA lifestyle.

Certainly a very strong middle class has grown up in Russia since the fall of communist Russia but Bird and Taurasi are experiencing an upper class lifestyle. They often times receive lucrative incentive bonuses, up to $5,000 during the season. They receive constant calls from their owner von Kalmanovic to be sure they are happy with their lifestyle. Bird and Taurasi have grown up faster than most 26 and 24 year olds. They have lived a lifestyle that few could ever envision growing up in the United States and playing on the cloistered campus of the University of Connecticut at Storrs. They earned it by the quality of their play and the fact that they are role models both on and off the court.

Diana Taurasi may be the greatest women's basketball player of all time. Auriemma would give you no argument on this. Paul Westhead, her coach for the

Phoenix Mercury would also give no argument. Summitt in all probability would agree as well. Count Vivian Stringer on that bandwagon as well.

Taurasi probably has not been as dominant in the WNBA as she was at UConn. But how could she possibly be? She won three consecutive National Championships at UConn and she is currently playing for one of the weakest WNBA teams. The only other star on the team is Cappie Pondexter from Rutgers.

Taurasi has averaged 19.4 ppg in largely a losing effort for Phoenix over a three year time span. Her shooting percentage is not as high as it was at UConn nor are her minutes per game.

Taurasi is probably playing in the right system in the WNBA under Westhead. It is a run and gun style that she is well suited for. It is not a style that Auriemma ran at UConn but it is a style built around her and her offensive prowess.

In three short years Taurasi has become accustomed to life in the WNBA and in Russia but fully acknowledges that "college is the best time in basketball. Nothing can top it. It was a lot of fun."

Taurasi clearly had the best time of her life playing at UConn and she fully acknowledges this fact. She was a superstar there and for her last couple of years was the only game in town. When Phoenix comes to the Mohegan Sun, a full hour away from UConn the stands are filled with UConn fans. Taurasi gets a standing ovation nearly every time she touches the ball.

She acknowledges unlike many other WNBA players that practices were actually more difficult in college than they are in the pros. Auriemma ran her into the ground and it started to wear on her body by March of each season. Taurasi only loss 8 games in college and fully expected to win every game for UConn. She no longer feels that way for Phoenix. She knows that it is not a reality given the parity that exists in the WNBA that still does not exist in the college game. She does appreciate the off season in the pros and mentioned that at schools like Tennessee and UConn there really is no off season and except for a stint playing for USA Basketball she trained all year long while she was at UConn.

Semeka Randall was one of the greatest players to ever play in Tennessee. Her game was based more on emotion than pure talent and she will admit that today.

Randall was drafted by Seattle of the WNBA right after college and played for Seattle, Utah and San Antonio. She once had 28 points in a WNBA game against Orlando.

Randall feels very strongly that a Program such as Tennessee prepares one for the WNBA more so than a lesser program.

She recognizes that it is still a difficult transition from college to pro just as it was from high school to college but the tools learned at Tennessee, especially in practice are valuable to both practices and games in the WNBA.

Randall noted that she was "constantly being challenged" at Tennessee and coach Summitt sat her on the bench if she was not ready to play. In the WNBA she was at times a scrub and her experience at Tennessee on the bench helped her learn to play that role as well.

Randall still marvels at the fact that she was getting paid to play in the WNBA and will never forget that experience and her life as a coach at West Virginia.

Tamika Catchings is one of the greatest Lady Vols of all-time. She may be the best. She is certainly the best athlete to ever play for Tennessee and that athleticism was evident not only at Tennessee but in the pros for Indiana Fever.

When Catchings entered Tennessee from Duncansville, Texas she was shy and introverted. Part of this came from a hearing loss which made her self conscious. She also played her first two years under the shadow of the great Chamique Holdsclaw. Holdsclaw was a star of those Tennessee teams and Catchings, although a great player played a subordinate role to her both on and off the court and as a leader.

Catchings really started to blossom as a junior and was the unquestioned team leader as a senior. She was the go to player. She might not have been the emotional leader that Randall was but she certainly was the most respected player on the team.

In 2002, her first year in the WNBA, she was the best player and the leader of the Fever and was named WNBA Rookie of the Year. She has led the Fever in points, rebounds, assists, steals and blocks in all 5 of her WNBA seasons.

In 2005 she scored her 2,000 point in the WNBA becoming the fastest player to score 2,000 career points. She is also the fastest to 1,000 rebounds, 400 assists and 300 steals. In 2005 and 2006 she was named the WNBA Defensive Player of the Year and was announced as a member of the All Decade Team along with nine other players.

Catchings is the daughter of former NBA player Harvey Catchings and her sister Tauja played at the University of Illinois.

Catchings recognizes that it really took her departure from Tennessee to blossom both as a person and as a leader. She had four great years at Tennessee but those years were regimented and exemplified by much time spent with her teammates both on and off the court. Things were dramatically different in Indiana. She says that the biggest adjustment to the WNBA is off the court and not on the court. She has to make her own schedule, find her own living arrangements and create her own social life. Most of that was done for her at Tennessee. She finds the players in the WNBA bigger, stronger and more talented but knows, without saying it that she is one of the best if not the best to ever play in the WNBA as well as in college. She looked up to Holdsclaw for her first two years and without sounding arrogant really had no one to look up to in the WNBA starting in 2002. Now she is respected both on and off the court by not only her teammates but fans of the Fever as well as the WNBA fans.

> *Brian Winters is a former NBA coach and a current WNBA coach. He coaches Catchings. He thinks that the biggest change from college to the pros, even from UConn or Tennessee is the difference in the rules. The fact that there is a backcourt, a 24 second clock and 4 quarters is a significant variance from the college rules from his perspective. He thinks that there is a big learning curve necessary in order to get accustomed to these new rules. He does admit that UConn and Tennessee, because of the spotlight that both Programs play in helps prepare their players for the WNBA better than most schools. He also feels that the players' size in the WNBA is a glaring difference from college even at the UConn and Tennessee level.*

THE RECRUITING WARS

For all the comparisons between the two programs on the national level, Tennessee and UConn have engaged in a scant number of recruiting battles against each other. It's never easy to discern how badly a program—any program—truly wants a player it doesn't get. Often, coaches will say they "backed off" at the end. In the cases of UConn and Tennessee, UConn has enjoyed more success than Tennessee in the head to head battles against each other but there are such a limited number of players who have come down to just UConn and Tennessee that it is impossible to say that one program recruits better than the other.

Just as UConn has really never recruited a high number of players from the southeast (Shea Ralph, Kalana Greene, Ketia Swanier), neither has Tennessee done a great deal in the northeast, save Chamique Holdsclaw and Nikki Anosike, both of New York.

Women's basketball on the collegiate level is different than men's basketball as women tend to go to school closer to home. It is not unusual to see men travel in droves from California to a locale such as Connecticut but women tend to make their ultimate college destinations more territorial. Sure Taurasi went to UConn from California and Holdsclaw went to Tennessee from New York but that is the exception rather than the rule.

Strangely UConn has probably had more heated recruiting wars with Rutgers than with Tennessee. Rutgers and UConn are both in the Big East and are situated in much closer geographic proximity and the ultimate decision by players such as Kia Vaughn, Cappie Pondexter, Asjha Jones, etc. have come down to Rutgers and UConn with Tennessee rarely if ever mentioned in their recruitment. Rutgers and UConn have battled each other on a relatively even basis over the past ten years or so and that is one of the reasons why they have split their last six games against each other.

Likewise for Tennessee the more common recruiting wars of late have been with schools with a southern geographic proximity such as Georgia, Duke or North Carolina. Tennessee has won most of those battles.

The Huskies, however, have the latest recruiting coup from the southeast, signing 2006 Naismith Award winner Maya Moore, a 6-foot forward from Suwanee, Ga., considered to be the best high school player in the country. Moore chose UConn over Tennessee, Georgia and Duke after a heated recruiting battle.

Moore held a press conference at Collins Hill High before last season even began to announce that she had chosen Connecticut.

"I really like the way they play, and they've put out some amazing talent the past few years," Moore told the New London Day, one of the many newspapers that covers UConn women's basketball. "Connecticut women's basketball is extremely popular in the North. It's something I'll look forward to, that love for basketball, just like I have. I can see myself doing a lot of good things at the university, both academically and athletically."

Players who choose between UConn and Tennessee often consider the cultural differences between living in the south and northeast. It's almost like the differences in personal backgrounds that have spiced up the Auriemma-Summitt relationship over the years.

Moore, who grew up in Jefferson City, Mo. And who lived for a while in Greensboro, N.C., had never lived in the north.

"It was something I had to think about: Would I be comfortable going that far away from the South?" said Moore. "But I'm OK with moving far from home. It's just a new challenge. I like putting myself in situations I've never been in before. Connecticut is definitely a situation I would take a chance on."

Many of Auriemma's players over the years have been quite comfortable not just around people, but around people much older than they are. Moore fits.

"I think obviously Maya's had some great schools to choose from," Collins Hill coach Tracey Tipton told the Hartford Courant, the state's largest daily newspaper. "I just think she felt best about Connecticut. Coach Auriemma did a great job recruiting her. She felt comfortable there. She really liked the style of play he uses within his program. She could flourish and fit in well with that type of system he runs at Connecticut. She also looked beyond just basketball. She wanted to go there because of their tradition. She knows she has a chance to not win just one national title but many. Maya is very gifted, has a great personality, very smart, a people person."

Ann Strother, who graduated from UConn with two National Championships, made up her mind during a snowstorm. She visited UConn from Colorado as a high school student and as the no. 1 high school player in the country in December of 2000, when nearly a foot of snow should have imperiled many UConn fans from filling the Hartford Civic Center for the UConn-Tennessee game.

Instead, the building was sold out, 16,294 strong. Many of the fans left home early and either took it slow, or spent the night at the Hilton Hotel, attached to the Civic Center.

Strother also chose UConn over Tennessee.

"I flew to Philadelphia and stayed with a friend there and then took the train up to Hartford," said Strother. "It was a good thing because it was a blizzard out and the roads were closed. Still, all those people found a way to the game when the city was shut down. I looked around and thought, 'How did these people get here?' It was so nasty outside. But the atmosphere and the intensity in the gym that day made me think, 'Wow, I really want to play here.'"

Strother had quite a visit to Tennessee but that did not dissuade her from attending UConn. Tennessee had t-shirts made up with Strother's baby picture on them and fans all over the campus wore them. Strother was touched by the display of affection at Tennessee but it wasn't enough to overcome her visit to UConn in the time that she spent with the UConn players. Summitt had thought that she was going to get Strother after her visit to Knoxville but UConn won out.

Tennessee, however, did get Semeka Randall, one of the best and most quotable players in program history. UConn recruited her as well. Auriemma, who has once irritated at something Randall said, once said of her, "She's a little cocky. I'll admit that's one of the reasons I recruited her."

Randall had good visits at both UConn and Tennessee but felt that Tennessee was more the place for her largely because of the tradition there at the time and the prospect of playing for Summitt, a coach she had looked up to for years. She made the decision to attend Tennessee on the last day of her visit there and then went home on Sunday evening and told her high school coach. She asked him to make the call to Auriemma but he said no it would be her responsibility. She was quite nervous and there was a reason for those nerves as the phone call with Auriemma didn't go well at all. He countered her at every turn when she tried to give the reasons for attending Tennessee and was nearly in tears at the end of the call. That is one of the many reasons that she took the UConn-Tennessee series so seriously and played some of the best games of her college career against UConn, hence earning her a spot earlier in this book as one of the top five players in the history of the UConn-Tennessee series. She clearly had something to prove to Auriemma after the phone call.

Randall and Shea Ralph, who chose UConn over Tennessee (among others) have both chosen the same career path: coaching.

Randall was part of Joanne P. McCallie's staff when McCallie took Michigan State to the Final Four in 2005.

"I'm excited about starting a new chapter in my life," Randall said at the time. "I'm walking away from playing the sport, but still part of the sport by giving back and helping kids. I've always believed this is what God had in store for me. I'm thrilled to be at MSU."

Randall played in the WNBA and overseas. At Tennessee, she was a Kodak All-American in 1999 and 2000. She played for Seattle (2001-02), Utah (2002) and San Antonio (2003-04), and also played in Israel (2001-02) and Greece (2002-03).

McCallie said of her, "She brings tremendous credibility as a national championship performer, a WNBA performer and a person committed to developing and mentoring people. Her enthusiasm, energy, commitment and focus were absolutely incredible from the very beginning. It is another example of our efforts to locate proven winners—people who have been where we want to go and people who can share stories about the process and the very exciting journey."

One of Randall's most challenging nights in coaching came the first time she coached against her old team at the 2005 Final Four. Michigan State, whose staff also had former Lady Vol assistant Al Brown, rallied to beat Tennessee and advance to the national championship game.

"It was definitely weird," Randall said. "I couldn't be [singing], 'Wish that I was on old Rocky Top …' I didn't even pay attention to it, I was so focused on what was going on and trying to stay in the moment."

Dan Fleser of the Knoxville News-Sentinel, asked McCallie after the game whether MSU had an advantage with Randall and Brown on the bench.

"Gosh, they didn't do a very good job if we were down 16," McCallie said. "No, I'm only kidding."

Randall told Fleser that couldn't believe Tennessee collapsed the way it did. "That was definitely different," she said. "Not like a normal Tennessee team—if they got up, they would sustain the lead and carry it to victory. And I know Pat's probably disappointed and heartbroken with what happened. "But it was great for our team, I was so ecstatic. I know that I'm blessed. People dream of being here."

Randall's presence within the MSU program gave McCallie a real-time example of what it takes to play professionally.

"I encourage her to show them what it takes," McCallie said. "It's hard to make the transition from a player to a coach. These young kids, they're very impatient, they want things to change overnight. But she's going to be a fantastic coach. She's energy personified."

Both Randall and McCallie recently left Michigan State. Randall first left to become an assistant at West Virginia and take on more recruiting responsibilities and McCallie left to become the head coach at Duke after Gail Goestenkors left for the Texas head job. Brown followed McCallie down to Duke as her primary tactician.

The easy decision for Shea Ralph would have been to go to Tennessee. Her mother Marsha Mann played with Pat Summitt in international competition in the mid 1970's and was a very good friend of hers. Because of that friendship Shea went to Tennessee camps for five consecutive years and felt that it was always her destiny to play at Knoxville for Summitt.

Tennessee took notice of her when she was only 11 years old and started to recruit her in earnest when she was a sophomore. Ralph really blossomed in her senior year and was named National High School Player of the Year by USA Today newspaper.

Starting with her junior year she considered not only Tennessee but also North Carolina, her home state as well as Connecticut. She knew intuitively that Connecticut was a budding power and wanted to visit the campus and meet head coach Auriemma. She had seen Connecticut beat Tennessee on television a number of times and was impressed with their hustle and their style as well as their winning way. They had a certain swagger that she really liked.

There was obviously a great deal of pressure on Ralph at home to go to Tennessee and in high school in Fayettville to go to North Carolina but it was Connecticut that was lurking in the back of her mind since 11th grade.

She paid a visit to Storrs in September of her senior year and her host player was Jen Rizzotti. She had watched Jen on television on many occasions and saw her on the cover of Sports Illustrated with the scintillating behind the back play that led UConn to its first National Championship with a win over Tennessee in 1995 in Minnesota. She knew that her style of play was similar to Rizzotti's and during the visit and after a number of meetings with not only Auriemma but Dailey and assistant coach Jamelle Elliot, she knew that Connecticut was a school for "blue collar" workers. She felt very much that she fit that style.

She verbaled to UConn during the visit. told associate head coach Dailey and called her mother from the airport in Hartford to tell her that. Her mother was surprised but did not try to talk her out of it. She wanted Shea to be an independent woman just like herself.

When Shea got home her mother told her that she had to contact both North Carolina and Tennessee personally. The call to North Carolina was not that difficult but the call to Tennessee was the toughest call of her life. When she finally got through to Summitt she blurted out the words that she was going to Connecticut. There was silence on the phone for awhile and then Summitt congratulated her on the decision and told her that she was sorry she was not going to Tennessee. She made no attempt to talk her out of her decision to go to UConn.

Ralph has never regretted the decision nor does she regret her 2000 National Championship ring.

Ralph is now a member of the Huskies of Honor, and a former National High School Player of the Year. She ended her career with the 2000 National Championship Most Outstanding Player award. It was a satisfying way to end a career that featured some painful knee injuries and a difficult decision even before her career began about whether she should attend UConn or Tennessee. There was much pressure on her to attend Tennessee as she was from the south (North Carolina) and her mother was very close friends with Summitt but her visit to UConn sold her on Auriemma and the prospects of playing for multiple National Championships.

Ralph has become part of the staff at the University of Pittsburgh, joining affable head coach Agnus Berenato. Pittsburgh made the NCAA Tournament in 2007 and even won a first-round game on its home floor before losing to eventual national champion Tennessee.

Ralph's post-UConn career has been quite enjoyable with Berenato, who Ralph called for a job at midnight. Here's the way it was recounted in the Hartford Courant:

"The night when Ralph called about Pitt's vacant assistant coaching job, Berenato was in her office, on the phone with her husband, Jack, learning about e-mail. It was close to midnight, and her secretary's phone rang. Berenato thought it might be her daughter, a college student. So she answered it.

'Good evening, women's basketball.'

There was a pause.

'Uh—what are you doing there?' the caller asked Berenato.

'Um, I work here,' she said.

'What are you doing calling me?'

'Well,' the words came in a rush, 'this is Shea Ralph and there was a job on the Internet and I'm interested in the job …'

Berenato said, 'Well, this is Agnus Berenato and if you're interested in that job, you'll be working here too at midnight.'

Ralph said, 'I thought I'd get a voicemail.' Berenato said, 'Well, this is what coaches do. We work this late at night.' Berenato told her husband she had to talk to Ralph. Something that she said piqued her interest. She was surfing the Internet. Not that Ralph is a computer geek, but with Berenato, she must have felt as if she were interviewing for a job with Microsoft. 'The questions I was asking her, I know she was probably shocked at,' Berenato says, laughing. 'Like, 'Do you know how to work a computer? Do you know how to do e-mail?' They talked until 1 in the morning. Ralph was hired a week later."

Ralph's job at Pittsburgh, like Randall's job at Michigan State and now West Virginia probably made them more sympathetic to Auriemma, Summitt, Chris Dailey and Mickie DeMoss. There's film-watching, scouting, writing recruiting letters, monitoring the players' academics.

Plus, she entered into a program that had to learn how to win.

"Geno had a certain way of doing things and it works," Ralph said. Agnes has said to me a few times, 'Shea, relax.' I say, 'Are you kidding me?'" Later, Ralph, speaking before a UConn-Pittsburgh game, said, "As a player at UConn, I learned how to do it their way or I left."

Ralph was very much in demand for certain head coaching jobs this past season and was directly contacted by Fairfield University in Connecticut. She didn't get the job but it won't be too long until she is a head coach, perhaps competing against both Auriemma and Summitt. And she is certainly a competitor.

TASS

When they were freshmen at UConn they did the unthinkable, they lost five games.

Some "greatest recruiting class ever," right?

When they were freshmen, there was a drought at the University of Connecticut and a harvest of players at Tennessee. Tamika Williams, Swin Cash, Asjha Jones, Sue Bird and Keirsten Walters, the greatest recruiting class Geno Auriemma or anyone ever assembled at UConn, actually began their careers with the earliest tournament exit the program had suffered since 1993. That year, 1999, the Huskies lost to Iowa State in the Sweet 16, the first time an Auriemma-coached team ever lost a regional semifinal.

Tennessee, meanwhile, was on course to win its fourth straight national championship. Chamique Holdsclaw, the centerpiece of the program, was about to go 4-for-4, four championships in four years, until one Monday night in March. Duke dethroned Tennessee in the regional final, unwittingly ending a Tennessee run—and beginning the greatest run in UConn history.

The next three years, Jones, Cash, Williams and Bird (injuries ended Walters' career early) made three Final Fours and won two national championships.

By the time of their real Senior Night of 2002, they had become legendary. And by the time of their real Senior Night, the night they made the Sweet 16 at Gampel Pavilion for the honest-to-goodness last home game, they had carved a place in program lore right there with the 1995 team that won the first championship. Truly the greatest recruiting class ever. Maybe four of the greatest players of all time.

That night in 2002 told the story as well as any other scene or anecdote could have, The story of "TASS," (Tamika, Asjha, Swin, Sue) began outside associate coach Chris Dailey's office the season before, 2001. Shea Ralph, sensing her time at UConn was on the back nine, became a bit wistful, telling Dailey, "I know it's never going to be like this again."

The "it" wasn't about the winning. The "it" was, is, and always will be about the constancy, comfort, and familial feelings provided by the program. From sisterhood in the locker room to Secret Santa gifts to pre-game scavenger hunts, the basketball always seems an admirable excuse to meet every day to bond and pursue a form of excellence, on and off the court.

And so along came the last time they'd really ever play at Gampel, when greatest recruiting class of them all faced reflection similar to Ralph's. As much as UConn Women's Senior Night has all but become a made for TV movie (UConn Senior Nights tend to be quite emotional), there was true finality here, melancholy wrapped around joy, at the thought of a goodbye on the night of the program's ninth straight trip to the Sweet 16.

Only in this program could "the girls' final home game" be a bigger storyline than a trip to the Sweet 16. That's the way it works here. The Sweet 16? Hell, the Huskymaniacs had already booked flights to the Final Four. But no more Swin, Tamika, Sue and Asjha? Now that's cause for a collective sigh.

At 10:38 p.m., March 18, 2002, the work of Sue Bird, Tamika Williams, Swin Cash and Asjha Jones was officially done in Storrs. Auriemma summoned them from the game and hugged them all. Williams, consistent with her personality, patted her coach on the head. And then when the game ended, they waved goodbye to 10,027 fans who have loved them unconditionally for four years, the way they loved Lobo, Rizzotti, Elliot, Wolters, Berube, Williams, Sales, Ralph, Hansmeyer and Abrosimova before them. They danced their way to the locker room. Then they came back for an encore.

And the fans still didn't leave, rhythmically clapping, awaiting another curtain call. The fans still come out to games at UConn in droves but not with the enthusiasm that they did when TASS was playing. There is no possible way for an encore. TASS simply had it all. The right players. The right ingredients. The right chemistry. And they were all fan favorites, especially Bird. Whenever Bird's Seattle Storm plays at Mohegan Sun in Connecticut there are droves of UConn fans there still after her for yet another autograph and another article of clothing. Bird is one of the all time fan favorites in the history of the University of Connecticut women's basketball.

They got it a few minutes later. Did Elvis ever get a second curtain call? Probably not. "James Brown," Williams said. "He always came back out." Williams said later, "I was sad at the end of the game, knowing I'd never be out there again. I tried to take it in before the game. The flags, the fans. At the end, it wasn't really a sad moment. The fans were so happy. The last thing I wanted was for them to see me cry. I'd rather smile."

And so should the fans. The program is resourceful, if nothing else. Greatest recruiting class of them all leaves ... another one enters. Or so everyone thought. A day before the final home game for four young people who delivered everything the outrageous hype said they would, Ann Strother, the headliner for next year, was named the Women's Basketball Coaches Association High School Player of the Year. Strother, Barbara Turner, Wilnett Crockett and Nicole Wolfe had signed on for the next season, four of the top 15 recruits in the country, while Gillian Goring, 6-foot-7 center whose ceiling was thought to be higher than Gampel's, was expected, finally, to fulfill her verbal commitment, giving the Huskies five more players over which the rest of the nation's coaches would either drool or shake their heads.

It's like the Huskies are on automatic product replenishment. The milk went sour? Suddenly, there's a tap-tap-tap at the back door ... and it's the milkman. Spilled wine on your best suit? Doorbell, honey. Why lookee here. It's the UPS man with a delivery from Brooks Brothers. Wolfe, Turner and Strother all played on state championship high school teams this winter, too. It would have done them good to watch the game on March 18, 2002, if for no other reason than to watch how Bird, Williams, Cash and Jones, heaped with the same expectations four years ago, have not only endured, but prevailed, quite triumphantly.

There was too much of the season left to dwell much on anything other than the hope and wonder that remained. And if national championship dreams weren't enough, there was a glimpse into what next season held. In a 40-second span, Diana Taurasi, a sophomore and at that point in time probably the best player in the country, made a left-handed scoop shot, a 3-pointer, and a Jordan fall-away, even though she was bumped before the shot.

You get the idea Taurasi has only given us the appetizer here the first two seasons, the clams casino before the veal chop.

Four young women you'll never forget finished their time in Storrs, while Pistol Pete and her posse awaited next season.

But did the coach draw up when he recruited these exceptional players and people along with Dailey that they would comprise four of the first six picks in the WNBA draft? Probably not. No one could have envisioned that.

Kevin McGuff is the head women's coach at Xavier and former chief recruiting assistant at Notre Dame. He recruited some of these players. He said that the true mark of greatness is not how heralded the players are when they come into a school but how heralded they are as seniors and as WNBA players. That is what really speaks from his prospective to the quality of a recruiting class. He is not interested in honors as a senior in high school but is more interested in honors for the players as seniors in college.

Bird was National College Player of the Year her senior year and she along with Williams, Cash and Jones were top picks in the WNBA draft. All four of them are still stars in the WNBA. She is said to have one of the keenest minds in all of women's college basketball. Ever wonder where that came from?

Do Auriemma and Dailey have an eye for talent? Most definitely but probably never more than in 1998 when he brought in TASS, the greatest recruiting class of all time, probably in the history of college basketball, men's or women's.

IS IT STILL THE GREATEST RIVALRY?

The question remains now given the fact that the teams don't play during the regular season whether or not the rivalry is as fierce as it once was. Also as important nationally.

The rivalry began as mentioned previously on January 16, 1995.

Tennessee's Pat Summitt had nothing to gain at the time. She had multiple National Championships and UConn had been to one Final Four in 1991 with no championships. Her vow though to play everyone anywhere and to help to bolster the women's game led her to accept a challenge from the Huskies to travel up to Gampel Pavilion on the campus of the University of Connecticut.

At the time the game was played the talent level at both UConn and Connecticut was relatively comparable. UConn had Rebecca Lobo whom many would consider the most significant recruit in UConn women's basketball history, Kara Wolters at 6'7" and star guard Jennifer Rizzotti. Tennessee had a strong cast as well led by point guard Michelle Marciniak. Tennessee was the glory school and UConn was the new kid on the block. No one familiar with women's college basketball at that time ever thought that UConn would surpass or come close to surpassing Tennessee on the national level. They were wrong.

UConn won not only the first game at Gampel but the national championship game in Minneapolis 70 to 64 behind the fiery play of Rizzotti. The rivalry had begun and it knew no bounds for the next seven or eight years.

In talking about those first two games Lobo recently said that "I have great memories of great games. The first one was the biggest game that I had played in my career at the time and the atmosphere was amazing. The arena was sold out and the crowd for about 15 minutes after the game was just dancing and celebrating in their seats. It was the best college basketball atmosphere I had ever experienced."

Since those games both teams have always been ranked in the top 15 nationally when they squared off including six times when they were actually 1-2 in the country.

Randall recently called it "one of the biggest games of the year." The question which remains on the table is whether or not the rivalry is as big today as it was in say 2000 when the teams played three games, one of which was for the national championship in Philadelphia before a sold out crowd and a national television audience.

Certainly to the purists the game is huge but does it draw in the casual basketball observer as much as it did say six or seven years ago? The answer is more complicated than just yes or no.

The two constants in the game remain. Auriemma and Summitt they are still the two best coaches in women's college basketball if not in all of college basketball. Both are now in the Women's Basketball Hall of Fame in Knoxville and in the Naismith Hall of Fame in Springfield. There are no greater honors in college basketball. Both are very distinct personalities. Auriemma is brash, intelligent and cocky. Summitt is very much of a lady. She would never make a public statement deriding another coach or program. When Auriemma had Taurasi he said quite publicly, "we've got Diana and you don't." Summitt refused to make a similar such comment about Candace Parker after the Lady Vols' win in January, 2007 in which Parker had 30 points and was dominant both inside and out and off the boards. She continues to make such a statement despite the fact that Parker won two straight National Championships.

It is impossible to talk about the game without talking about Geno and Pat. Would the game have as much panache without Geno and Pat on the sidelines? Debby Jennings, the Sports Information Director and Associate Athletic Director at University of Tennessee feels that it would. She has been at Tennessee for 30 years and has witnessed every UConn-Tennessee clash. She feels that the game is big enough to even overshadow the coaching greatnesses of Geno and Pat and stands on it's own as one of the greatest college rivalries of all time. She does add though that while UConn has Tennessee as its predominant rival and Rutgers as a rival to a lesser extent, Tennessee has a number of rivalries which have grown over the years and that serves on certain levels to mitigate the absolute importance of the UConn game. Old Dominion is a long standing rival with Tennessee as is Texas and Stanford. In the SEC Georgia is a huge rivalry and there is even a coaching rivalry as a sub plot with Andy Landers of Georgia and Summitt. Tennessee at one point in time had a huge rivalry with in state foe Vanderbilt when Jim Foster was at the helm at Vanderbilt but Foster has since moved on to Ohio State and Vanderbilt has fallen on some hard times basketball wise.

Al Brown, former assistant at Tennessee and current assistant at Duke feels that the rivalry would fall off a bit without Geno and Pat as they are the two most charismatic coaches in the game today. He feels very much that the rivalry has benefited UConn more than it has benefited Tennessee as it has really helped to catapult UConn up in the polls. He was never a big fan of starting the series from the get go.

Rutgers had a three game winning streak against UConn and Auriemma heading into February of 2007 and it may be the game that Auriemma and his team wants to win the most for two very distinct reasons. First it is a Big East Conference game and they always overshadow out of conference games and secondly Rutgers is a team which UConn most often competes for recruits and is most often over the past five or six years lost players to. The most notable loss for Auriemma in that recruiting rivalry is former star Rutgers player and current Phoenix Mercury WNBA star Cappie Pondexter.

There is no doubt that the game has tremendous significance to the alumni players of both schools but in interviews with players from Tennessee and UConn it appears to have even more significance to the Connecticut players.

Early 1990's Connecticut player Healy doesn't go to many women's college basketball games due to a very busy career as an executive at Merck, but rarely if ever misses the UConn-Tennessee game either in person or on television. That is her Super Bowl of women's college basketball. The same holds true with Rizzotti. She is the highly successful coach at the University of Hartford but if her team is not playing no matter where she is she will make time to watch the game on CBS. Bird and Taurasi for the past two years have been playing winter ball in Russia at the time of the UConn-Tennessee game but both do their best to listen to it on the computer feed.

Catchings has a little bit different take on the game. She still cares about it and still cares about her Tennessee affiliation but she has missed many of the games since her graduation. She wants Tennessee to be successful and to win the game but it is no longer the be all and end all of her basketball existence. Randall is now an assistant coach at Michigan State University, a women's powerhouse. Her team had a game at number 1 Maryland just preceding the UConn-Tennessee game and she got a call from her mother a few days before both games asking her what she thought about the big game. She immediately responded about the Maryland-Michigan State game and her mother expressed to her that she was referring exclusively to the UConn-Tennessee game. It would appear that old habits die hard.

Tasha Butts is currently an assistant at Duquesne under former Tennessee Associate Head Coach Mickie DeMoss. Her team is starting to develop a strong SEC resume but she still recognizes that UConn-Tennessee is *the game*. She feels that the rivalry was somewhat more heated in the early 2000's because one or the other team was coming off a National Championship but even this year, on her way back to Kentucky from a game at Ohio State she kept calling for score updates. Butts says it is impossible to take the Geno-Pat subplot out of the game especially in the eyes of the media but says that the game is bigger than both coaches at this point in time.

Kyra Elzy is now an assistant at Kansas. She has a friendly rivalry with Kansas athletic director Lew Perkins who was once the athletic director at UConn. On the day of the UConn-Tennessee game this past season they both kidded each other about the outcome of the game. Elzy feels that the game is great for young kids as they identify almost from birth with either UConn or Tennessee and kids at the top of the high school game still always consider one of those two storied Programs at the top of their favorite list when choosing their ultimate playing destination. She recruits kids to Kansas who show up for their recruiting visit wearing some sort of Tennessee paraphernalia. It gives her a lot of pride but makes the recruiting process even more difficult for her.

From 1995 through at least 2004 there was no greater rivalry in women's college basketball if not in all of college basketball than UCONN—Tennessee. It garnered some of the greatest ratings on ESPN and captivated the nation's basketball fans whenever the game was played.

Has that situation changed at all and if so why?

There are varying opinions on the topic with a host of underlying rationals for each.

Catchings feels that the rivalry was at such a fever pitch in the late 1990's that it was bound to wear off and indeed has succumbed to both Conference and in state as well as regional rivalries. She recognizes that Rutgers—Connecticut may be a bigger game to UConn than Tennessee and feels that now many Tennessee players and coaches are fixated on beating North Carolina and Duke out of Conference and Georgia in Conference.

Rizzotti does not agree. She indicates that there may be more parity in the women's game right now, but there still isn't and may never be a rivalry like UConn—Tennessee. She said that at the end of this past season that "no matter where I am if I'm not coaching on the bench that day I will watch the game." She spends a great deal of time during the week of the game communicating with players like Healy, a former teammate by email about what she expects to happen between the two teams and even places an occasional call to Auriemma or Dailey during that week to wish her former coaches luck. Her sentiment is echoed by Taurasi, who also tries to stop in her tracks on the day of the game, even if she is playing in Europe to catch it live either on television or the internet. That was the case in 2006 for both her and Bird who were both playing in Russia but had enough time to catch the game on the internet.

Coach Goestenkors, formerly of Duke and now of Texas whose program has probably elevated more than any other since the advent of the UConn-Tennessee series still feels that the game is the premiere game in women's college basketball and it's a must see for not only prospective players and current players but coaches throughout the nation. She has never missed one on television when she is not actually coaching a game and has every expectation of watching the game again this coming year.

McGuff of Xavier feels that the rivalry is as big as ever because of Geno and Pat. He cites them as being the two most charismatic coaches in the country and probably the two best coaches. He does recognize that with more parity nationally there are great players at a few dozen schools including his own but says that the world of women's college basketball really stops on a dime the day of the UConn-Tennessee game and everyone wants to see who will win it to get a true measure of what things will look like nationally in March. Does he think that the rivalry will change when either Geno or Pat or both of them are no longer at their respective schools. He is not sure but for the time being it is a game that he certainly will never miss on television if he is available to watch it.

NEXT SEASONS

So what if anything did we learn from 2006-07 that will be instructive for future years for both UConn and Tennessee, as well as women's basketball in the national scene?

We know that there are four teams entering next season that will be stronger than everyone else. LSU returns all their starters but has a new head coach in Van Chancellor. Chancellor has not coached college women's college basketball since 1997 when he was the head coach of Mississippi. He served the next ten years as head coach of the Houston Comets of the WNBA. The women's game has changed dramatically in the past ten years so one question has to be asked is how you will react to the changes in the players and the game.

Rutgers returned all of their starters and brought in an All-American point guard from Wilmington, Delaware by the name of Khadijah Rushdan. She was slotted to be a starter right from the get go. Unfortunately she was injured her freshman season. The question that remains open for Rutgers is whether or not their offense will be high octane enough to withstand four grueling NCAA games at the end of the season. UConn, as Rutgers returns all their starters and brings in whom many perceive to be one of the truly great high schoolers of all time in Maya Moore of Georgia. Moore was the Unanimous National Player of the Year and helped her team, Collins Hill to an undefeated season and a no. 1 ranking nationally. Tennessee returns Parker and Hornbuckle and a cast of many others from a National Championship team and they also had yet another great recruiting class under Summitt. They bring in 6-4 forward Victoria Baugh from Sacramento who is a first team USA Today All-American, Angie Bjorklund from Spokane, Washington, a 6-1 guard who is also a USA Today First Team All-American. The rich certainly get richer.

Duke, North Carolina, Notre Dame, Marquette, Baylor, Purdue, Stanford and a host of other schools will be powerful next season and all will have a chance at an Elite Eight berth, if not a Final Four appearance. One of the distinguishing characteristics will be the numerous coaching changes which could impact on team chemistry. Duke lost head coach Gail Goestenkors to Texas and brought in Michigan State head coach Joanne McCallie. She had transformed Michigan State into an elite program and she can keep the beat running at Duke.

Parity was mentioned previously as still reigning supreme in the women's game but the fact of the matter is that both UConn and Tennessee will once again be at the top of the polls next year and presumably for years to come. Is this fact compatible with parity? Many in the know feel that the answer to this question is yes.

She cites the fact that Maryland won a National Championship two years ago and that Baylor recently won one and that schools like Duke have been oh so close in the past few years to winning it all.

Jamelle Elliot, UConn assistant coach and former Husky great from Washington, D.C. truly believes that the parity now in the women's game is far more significant than it has ever been in the past and feels that parity is still compatible with UConn and Tennessee still being at the highest level.

She does agree though that UConn and Tennessee are at the top and should remain at the top for a variety of reasons. She feels very firmly that Geno and Pat are the two finest coaches in the land and that many top kids simply want to play for one or both of them right from when they first pick up a basketball. They are the two most televised teams and this adds to their exposure nationally to young players. She also feels that kids right now are very impatient and want to win National Championships as soon as possible and that these very same future college players know that either or both teams will be competing for a National Championship year in and year out. The same can't be said for the other schools mentioned by Elliot to the author in her analysis of parity in the women's game today.

Marianne Stanley is the nation's 19th winningest women's college basketball coach of all time. She helped Old Dominion to three National Championships as the head coach. She is currently an assistant at Rutgers under Stringer and feels that there are many teams inching closer to UConn and Tennessee. She would not be surprised if Rutgers and LSU are rated higher than UConn and Tennessee going into 2007-08. She does feel that the tradition over the past decade at both UConn and Tennessee is a big advantage for both schools.

Carlene Mitchell is also an assistant at Rutgers and feels that there is far more parity in the women's game today than ever in the past. She does feel though that the television exposure for both UConn and Tennessee gives them an advantage and admitted that on the day of the UConn-Tennessee game if she is not coaching she will watch that game intently and the same might not be said for another top women's game also being televised.

Tasha Pointer, an assistant at Rutgers was a high school All-American and played at Rutgers. She was also recruited by UConn and feels that parity in the women's game has changed dramatically over the past five years. She thinks that far more financial resources are being put into athletic budgets by athletic directors from throughout the country so as to permit other teams to compete nationally with the UConn's and Tennessee's of this world. She cites the $950,000 a year salary for seven years that Stringer at Rutgers was recently awarded by Athletic Director Bob Mulcahy. That makes Stringer the fourth highest paid coach in a game behind Summitt, Auriemma and Goestenkors.

Chris Golbrecht, current Yale head coach and former women's head coach at USC and Florida State was a bit more analytical in her approach to the UConn-Tennessee series and its impact on parity. She noted that the more television exposure given to other teams the less that Tennessee and UConn seem bigger than life. She thought that it was quite telling that coach Summitt didn't win a National Championship between 1998 and 2007 and in the interim programs such as Rutgers, Duke, North Carolina and Notre Dame burgeoned. She concluded by saying that:

> "Pat and Geno are like Microsoft and Boeing—there are tremendous benefits to be gained from getting the formula right early, establishing the standard, staying in one place and never losing your edge. Other Programs took tumbles because one of those requirements didn't apply. Pat and Geno have to be considered the leaders in their field, but they are not only great coaches out there. They are however, the ones smart enough to know that they had found their niche and built their kingdoms and those are not easy things to do anymore in this day and age."

The greatest rivalry in the history of women's sports, UConn-Tennessee ended abruptly in early June, 2007 and I broke the story.

It all happened in late April 2007 when I got a note from a former SEC assistant that the series was coming to an end. I thought that this coach was nuts. Off the wall. But he insisted its truth and I had to follow it up, not only for the sake of the book but for the sake of my own cusiousity. Was it UConn? Was it Tennessee? Was it a combination of the two. Had the television contract fallen apart. All of these resonated in my head. I got no comment from UConn. No comment from Tennessee and someone as close to both of these coaches as Harry Perretta of Villanova seemed to know nothing.

I spoke with Catchings, Healy, Strother, Randall and a host of others. No one knew and most basically told me that it was impossible. That the game was too big for an individual, entity or institution to cause it to end. So I basically gave up on that topic. Gave up until I went to a Liberty game in early June. I ran into Taurasi and we spoke about the transition from the college game to the WNBA. We had a good chat and then at the end as she was running out to the court she winked at me and said "Don't be so sure that the game is going to continue and the bad guys ended it." Then I knew. I knew for sure.

I then spoke to Mel Greenberg and he was still skeptical but he was on his way down to Tennessee for his induction ceremony into the Women's Basketball Hall of Fame and said that he would look into it. He called me on June 7 and said "something is up. "I couldn't reach him back but I knew what he meant. Summitt, Jennings and AD Joan Cronan weren't talking. Jennings said that the SEC did not permit talk about schedules before July 1. That meant nothing to me because all that Tennessee had to do was to affirm that the series was continuing. They didn't. A contract was sitting on Cronan's desk to continue the series for two more years and it wasn't signed. Stiff had made a rather strange trip down to Knoxville to talk to Tennessee about the series. Tennessee had reported UConn on what they claimed was a recruiting violation in January. It all added up to me. It was over.

I write for SI.Com and really respect them and the magazine. I contacted their editor BJ Schecter on the evening of June 7 and told him what I knew. He said that he would look into it. I got an urgent e-mail from him at 3:13 pm the next day. By the time I got back to him the story was already up. It was written by Richard Deitsch. I was glad that it was written by him. He knew women's basketball. The story was written at 4:45 and amended later after 6:00 when Hathaway made a statement that the series was over because Tennessee would not sign the contract. It was hard for Jeff to knock Tennessee because the President of Tennessee was a friend of his and a former Dean at UConn. But he had to protect his coach. Cronan basically said the series was over with no explanation. Summitt and Auriemma said nothing. Summitt was busy with the Induction ceremony in Knoxville. Greenberg among others was being inducted. ESPN.com followed suit with a story about the series and then it became major news that night and all weekend. Everywhere.

Dan Flesser is the number one beat writer for Tennessee for the Knoxville News. It was his stated job to be covering the Induction ceremony. At least he thought so until the news boke on June 8. He stopped everything and wrote about the series. It dwarfed all other stories in Connecticut and Tennessee. Sports and news.

UConn issued a statement from its athletic department, stipulating that the decision came from Tennessee. Later, Tennessee women's athletic director Joan Cronan issued the statement, "Tennessee has elected not to renew its series with the University of Connecticut. The Lady Vol basketball team will continue to enjoy its rivalry games with teams from the Big East, the ACC, the Big 12, the Pac-10 and other conferences. Year in and year out, we pride ourselves on the strength of schedule we play and our RPI." Tennessee coach Summitt didn't say why Tennessee decided to end the rivalry and continues not to say such, but there is speculation that it is over some recruiting issues she had with Auriemma with respect to Moore. UConn coach Geno Auriemma wouldn't speak for the record about it.

The consensus, though, was that the decision to end the series that had done so much to promote women's sports was a major blow to the growth of all women's sports in general. This was the only women's game CBS made sure it televised every year, always the first Saturday in January.

The games obviously provided a litany of memories. They began, as stated previously, on Martin Luther King Day in 1995 when UConn won what was then the biggest game in program history and became No. 1 for the first time. Three months later, the Huskies beat the Lady Vols again in the National Championship game and became a true rival.

Tennessee got revenge during a classic overtime game at the 1996 Final Four. In 1999, there was Semeka Randall rolling around the floor with Svetlana Abrosimova, much to the chagrin of the UConn crowd. That day earned Randall the nickname that stuck with her: "Boo."

In 2000, UConn fans showed up to Hartford en masse, despite a snowstorm, months after the Huskies beat Tennessee in the national championship game. In

2002, Diana Taurasi punched the basket stanchion at Thompson-Boling Arena because she wanted to hit "something orange" en route to scoring 32 points. Taurasi made a 65-footer a year later.

Candace Parker dunked in 2007 at the Hartford Civic Center, giving Tennessee its ninth win against 13 losses in the series.

And the memories were supposed to live on, until the Lady Vols ended the series. "The question I have is 'why?'" UConn grad and Connecticut Sun forward Asjha Jones said of the rivalry's end. "It's a special game. Just like the games we have with Detroit (in the WNBA). It brings out extra emotion."

"The chance to play Tennessee was the most exciting thing, because that was *the* game," UConn grad Swin Cash told the Hartford Courant. "To get to the National Championship you realized you probably had to go through one of us. And (the game) was a big recruiting tool for kids who wanted to play for the championship; either you go to UConn or you go to Tennessee."

Cash continued, "That's like saying that Duke and North Carolina (men) aren't going to play anymore. It has become such a premier game in college basketball, and not just for basketball fans, but any kind of athlete. You ask them about rivalries and they know all about Duke-North Carolina and Connecticut-Tennessee. I'm sad to see it come to this. I am certain that the growth of women's basketball will produce other teams to come onboard. But I don't think anyone will ever forget how much that game did for the sport." "Honestly, I think it's a shame," University of Hartford coach Jen Rizzotti, a UConn grad, told the Courant. "No matter how many nationally ranked teams UConn has on its schedule, the Tennessee game has always had a special feeling and excitement about it."

The end of the rivalry left Connecticut fans with only Rutgers and the Detroit Shock remaining as chief rivals of their basketball teams.

Two days after the Tennessee-UConn series ended, the Shock came to Mohegan Sun Arena. Detroit coach Bill Laimbeer, already unpopular with the Sun fans from his days playing against the Celtics, emerged from a hallway and into Mohegan Sun Arena, smirking as the concert of boos rained on him.

Then the game began. There were three technical fouls in the first 14 minutes. A flagrant foul on Margo Dydek. Laimbeer later told the media that "Margo tried to hurt" Swin Cash. Bodies hit the floor like bowling pins. Players and coaches shrieked at the officials. Leather-lunged Jamie Tarr, Sun forward Kristen Rasmussen's husband, delivered an absorbing, "Hey, Laimbeer, sit down and shut up!" some time in the second half.

"We enjoy playing here," Laimbeer said. "We enjoy getting the crowd involved. We enjoy being the bad guys. In this league, this is the biggest spot, not only for myself, but as a ballclub, where they don't care for us."

Later, Laimbeer addressed the end of the Connecticut-Tennessee rivalry. "Maybe nobody likes playing in Connecticut," he said. "I don't think the (end of the) Connecticut-Tennessee rivalry will have any impact on the sport whatsoever," Laimbeer said. "There's some great women's college basketball. Other rivalries are developing. Don't hold on to the past. Tennessee's not upset. Just you guys (the Connecticut writers) up here. So what?"

Fans and media in both markets beamoned the end of the rivalry, too. From New London Day columnist Mike DiMauro: "It's the rivalry. Are you paying attention so far, coach Summitt? The rivalry. You remember that, don't you? The rivalry with UConn? That thing responsible for taking women's basketball more mainstream? For taking *you* more mainstream? What, like anybody really cared about you before you went head-to-head with Geno?"

From columnist John Adams of the Knoxville-News Sentinel: "This is the biggest rivalry in women's basketball. Nothing else is close. Yet Summitt is ending it without comment. Imagine Summitt assigning no one to guard Diana Taurasi in the Final Four, then offering no explanation in the postgame press conference. This makes even less sense.

The Lady Vols aren't just sticking it to UConn. They're sticking it to their own fans. Their three biggest home crowds have all come against UConn, the team UT fans love to beat. Ending the series affects more than UT and UConn. It affects all of women's basketball. It affects the networks, too.

"So why back out of a series that has meant so much to your program, your fans and your sport? And without further explanation, the story won't go away. It will come up repeatedly and will be magnified if the teams meet in the NCAA tournament. No one should understand that better than Summitt, who is as media savvy as anyone in the business. But she is dismissing the Huskies as casually as she might cancel a preseason game with the Houston Jaguars. UConn deserves better than that. So does women's basketball."

From Hartford Courant columnist Jeff Jacobs: You don't kill the greatest rivalry in a sport without explanation. You just don't. Summitt is going down as the soberest of cowards. She has quit on the greatest rivalry in women's sports. She has delivered a haymaker to college basketball…. Could you imagine if USC pulled the plug on its football rivalry with Notre Dame and Pete Carroll refused to say why? Or Army quitting on Navy?

Together, Tennessee and UConn have lifted women and sports. "… Is this about Pat not having enough control? Is Pat worn out by the annual circus? She was the one behind dropping the series from two games a year to one. And now she's behind it disappearing. When the Vols made the trip to Hartford over the winter, 2007 there were a few comments from the Tennessee camp that they may have had enough. "Has fencing with Geno worn her out? Has the excitement and occasional contentiousness of the rivalry become too much for her? Or does she figure that Geno has more to gain by playing her than she has playing Geno? After all, Tennessee can sell the SEC and the fertile basketball of the South. If that's the case, isn't that selfishness on Pat's part? Little girls dream about playing in the UConn-Tennessee game. Fans from all over love it, and look at all the glory brought to the Tennessee girls from the rivalry. It's the centerpiece of the sport. The game isn't about Pat or Geno. Yet Pat Summitt is killing the series. And two words come to mind. Craven. Selfish. We never thought we'd say that about Pat Summitt. Never." What is really lost is the fact that UConn and Tennessee will play again. They will play in the NCAA's in 2008 or another season. They are the two best teams going into 2007. It is inevitable that they will meet and the stakes, pressure and notoreity will even be higher. The game will be lost in the chatter. It will be all about what happend in June 2007. It will be all about the end of the series yet again. It won't be about Moore, Tina Charles, Renee Montgomery or Parker. It will be about Auriemma and Summitt. But maybe in a strange was that is who it should really be about because if nothing else I learned in writing this book that it is as much Auriemma-Summitt as it is UConn-Tennessee. And it took that toxic combination to end the series just like it took their charisma to start it. As Yogi Berra would have said "it ain't over until it's over." And it's not over. Maybe.

EPILOGUE

So what have we learned from all these chapters, words and anecdotes about UConn and Tennessee? Well, we know that they are still the two premiere women's basketball teams and programs in the country and that this hegemony is not going to end for a long time. Certainly not this season. No team is even close to either of them at this juncture. No team has won more than one National Championship since Tennessee started its unbelievable run and most of the teams that have won National Championships have had many miserable seasons since then.

Tennessee had the best player in the country on its team last season in Candace Parker and she will not return. UConn added Maya Moore the daughter of former Rutgers great Mike Dabney and she had a great freshman season and will be bringing in Elena Della Donne from Delaware next year. That will give them the top three prep players of the year in a row in Charles, Moore and Della Donne.

Why is it that Duke, North Carolina, Rutgers, LSU, Bayler, Notre Dame, Purdue, etc. have not had staying power? Well, there appear to be a number of reasons. They have all had great recruiting classes but they haven't had great recruiting classes year in and year out. Many of these programs have lost players to transfer, etc. More importantly they both lack the key element that has kept UConn and Tennessee on the map. That element is the charismatic, talented and skilled head coach at the level of Auriemma and Summitt. That is not to say that Stringer, McGraw, etc. are not great coaches. They are. They are both Hall of Fame coaches but between them they have only won one National Championship. Auriemma and Summit now have 12 with at least a couple of more on the horizon. They are both Federer and Woods like in terms of winning majors.

We also know that the name Tennessee or the name UConn on a players shirt dictates to a large extent their basketball self-esteem, readiness to play and feeling about the ultimate outcome of the game. Tennessee and UConn players to a person simply feel that they will win every game they suit up for. It is something inculcated in them once they step onto the picturesque campuses in Nashville and Storrs and is a concept that never leaves them throughout the four years or so of playing time.

2006-07 was an excellent example of the strengths of the Tennessee and UConn names. Neither team was ranked preseason no. 1 and both were considered long shots to win a National Championship given the strength of Duke, the fact that defending National Champion Maryland returned all of its starters and the powerhouse in Chapel Hill, North Carolina led by Ivory Latta. Well as we know Tennessee did win a National Championship despite a few hiccups along the road and UConn made it to another Elite Eight on the strength of a bunch of freshman and sophomores.

Tennessee went into the National Championship game against a not so big underdog Rutgers team expecting to win. Many thought that Rutgers was content after their huge win against LSU in just making it to the National Championship game after starting the season 2-4. Well anyone who knows Stringer knows that that is not the case but at least in the beginning of the game Rutgers appeared to be tentative and Tennessee was hitting the boards, their trademark with abandon. Tennessee built up a big lead and Rutgers simply did not have the offense that day to match them basket for basket. They probably left a lot of their offense on the court against LSU to nights before in Cleveland.

An interesting development unrelated to the Programs at Tennessee and UConn took place on the way to the publication of this book. The now infamous Don Imus comments about the Rutgers basketball team took place in April, 2007. It brought not only race relations and the plight of women to the national forefront but also on certain levels brought women's basketball into people's consciousness. Rutgers appeared on the cover of Newsweek and other magazines and when was the last time that one of the major news magazines had a women's basketball team on the cover?

Interestingly people started to talk about women's basketball on news shows, radio programs and television programs throughout the country. We got to hear not only about the exploits of the Rutgers team in the sports pages but also the front pages of most newspapers, magazines and internet sites.

Summitt issued extensive comments about Imus and Rutgers as follows:

> *I was in disbelief. I have never heard anyone be so disrespectful. Vivian has some wonderful student-athletes who represent the game. I was disturbed when I read the remarks. These are young adults who are wonderful role models, women of impact. We are talking 2007."*

Auriemma made no official comments for the record but did note that he is no fan of Imus.

Most internet sports boards were totally supportive of Rutgers and the plight of its athletes. Tennessee was especially supportive. The UConn board, UConnfan.com was consistently far less than complimentary about Rutgers and Stringer. They echoed the comments of writer Jason Whitlock who said that "Stringer was looking for her 15 minutes of fame." In reality Stringer has had far more than 15 minutes of fame in her fabled coaching career and certainly never asked for Imus to issue the remarks that he did about her team.

Women's college basketball was in good hands heading into 2007-08. Rutgers beat Maryland in the annual Jimmy V. Classic in November before a national television audience.

The season played out according to schedule but UConn and Tennessee did not meet for the National Championship. Tennessee behind an injured but very game Parker made it to the Final Four along with Stanford, LSU and UConn. Stanford beat UConn and Tennessee edged out LSU and then beat Stanford 64-48 for the National Championship in Tampa.

Auriemma in a postseason press conference blasted Summitt for canceling the series and not telling the public directly the reason, namely that she contended that UConn had violated certain recruiting rules in the recruitment of Moore.

ESPN has already committed to televise more games than it did in the past under the fine leadership of Stiff. The game is in good shape.

TOP 25 ALL-TIME LARGEST HOME CROWDS IN TENNESSEE HISTORY

	CROWD	OPPONENT	RESULT	DATE
1.	24,653	CONNECTICUT	89-80 W	1/7/06
2.	24,611	CONNECTICUT	72-86 L	1/5/02
3.	24,597	CONNECTICUT	84-69 W	1/3/98
4.	24,563	Texas	78-97 L	12/9/87
5.	24,373	Old Dominion	85-61 W	2/7/98
6.	24,051	Kentucky	98-60 W	1/7/99
7.	24,046	CONNECTICUT	92-88 W	2/1/01
8.	23,385	CONNECTICUT	67-74 L	1/8/00
9.	22,694	Louisiana State	90-58 W	2/22/98
10.	22,635	Georgia	102-69 W	1/14/99
11.	22,515	CONNECTICUT	67-81 L	2/5/04
12.	21,968	Vanderbilt	70-66 W	2/22/01
13.	21,592	Vanderbilt	64-59 W	2/17/97
14.	21,077	Mississippi State	94-53 W	2/6/99
15.	20,956	Vanderbilt	75-68 W	2/16/02
16.	20,790	Florida	93-95 L (OT)	2/26/06
17.	20,573	Kentucky	89-64 W	2/24/02
18.	20,090	Louisiana State	85-62 W	2/29/04
19.	20,068	Vanderbilt	89-53 W	2/18/99

	CROWD	OPPONENT	RESULT	DATE
20.	19,722	UCLA	100-77 W	12/21/98
21.	19,576	Louisiana State	69-72 L	2/9/06
22.	19,339	Alabama	65-47 W	2/6/00
23.	19,208	Vanderbilt	86-54 W	1/25/98
24.	19,143	Kentucky	83-39 W	1/27/01
25.	18,643	Vanderbilt	72-63 W	2/13/05

COLLEGE BASKETBALL'S BEST RIVALRIES

Rivalries—A number of websites and articles have published what they consider to be the greatest college basketball rivalries of all time. Many differ. The one found in www.collegehoopsnet.com is very interesting and instructive as it relates to this book as follows:

1. Duke—North Carolina (Men)

   It just never gets old. So much tradition, talent and success at both schools. It's the best, no doubt about it.

2. UCONN-TENNESSEE (Women)

   People would find it hard to argue this one. These teams are playing for championships and number 1 rankings every time they lace them up.

3. Xavier-Cincinnati (Men)

   They haven't played many games decided by more than 10 points.

4. Kansas-Missouri (Men)

   There's a reason the Big 12 make sure they play twice every year.

5. Duke-Maryland (Men)

   Definitely one of the better rivalries of the last four-five years. This one is only going to get better.

1999-00 AP

1. CONNECTICUT
2. TENNESSEE
3. Louisiana Tech
4. Georgia
5. Notre Dame
6. Penn State
7. Iowa State
8. Rutgers
9. Santa Barbara
10. Duke
11. Texas Tech
12. Mississippi State
13. Purdue
14. Old Dominion
15. LSU
16. Auburn
17. Boston College
18. Oklahoma
19. Virginia
20. Oregon
21. Arizona
22. Tulane
23. NC State
24. Xavier
25. Michigan

2000-01 AP

1. CONNECTICUT
2. Notre Dame
3. TENNESSEE
4. Georgia
5. Duke
6. Louisiana Tech
7. Oklahoma
8. Iowa St.
9. Purdue
10. Vanderbilt
11. Rutgers
12. Xavier
13. Texas Tech
14. Florida
15. SW Missouri St.
16. Iowa
17. Utah
18. LSU
19. No. Carolina St.
20. Colorado
21. Penn St.
22. Clemson
23. Baylor
24. Wisconsin
25. Arizona St.
26. Virginia Tech

2001-02 AP		2002-03 AP	
1.	CONNECTICUT	1.	CONNECTICUT
2.	Oklahoma	2.	Duke
3.	Duke	3.	LSU
4.	Vanderbilt	4.	TENNESSEE
5.	Stanford	5.	Texas
6.	TENNESSEE	6.	Louisiana Tech
7.	Baylor	7.	Texas Tech
8.	Louisiana Tech	8.	Kansas State
9.	Purdue	9.	Stanford
10.	Iowa State	10.	Purdue
11.	Kansas St.	11.	Villanova
12.	Colorado	12.	North Carolina
13.	South Carolina	13.	Mississippi State
14.	Texas	14.	Vanderbilt
15.	Old Dominion	15.	Penn State
16.	North Carolina	16.	South Carolina
17.	Texas Tech	17.	Minnesota
18.	Minnesota	18.	Santa Barbara
19.	Cincinnati	19.	Georgia
20.	Colorado St.	20.	Ohio State
21.	Boston College	21.	Wisconsin-GB
22.	LSU	22.	Arizona
23.	Florida Int.	23.	Rutgers
24t.	Florida	24.	Arkansas
24t.	Penn St.	25.	Boston College
		25.	George Washington

2003-04 AP		2004-05 AP	
1.	Duke	1.	Stanford
2.	TENNESSEE	2.	LSU
3.	Purdue	3.	TENNESSEE
4.	Texas	4.	North Carolina
5.	Penn St.	5.	Duke
6.	CONNECTICUT	6.	Baylor
7.	Louisiana Tech	7.	Michigan State
8.	Kansas St.	8.	Ohio State
9.	Houston	9.	Rutgers
10.	Stanford	10.	Notre Dame
11.	Oklahoma	11.	Texas
12.	North Carolina	12.	Minnesota
13.	Vanderbilt	13.	CONNECTICUT
14.	Texas Tech	14.	Texas Tech
15.	Baylor	15.	Temple
16.	Georgia	16.	DePaul
17.	Colorado	17.	Kansas State
18.	Boston College	18.	Iowa State
19.	LSU	19.	Vanderbilt
20.	TCU	20.	N.C. State
21.	Ohio St.	21.	Georgia
22.	Auburn	22.	Penn State
23.	Michigan St.	23.	Boston College
24.	Minnesota	24.	Wisc-Green Bay
25.	Villanova	25.	TCU

2005-06 AP

1. North Carolina
2. Ohio State
3. Maryland
4. Duke
5. LSU
6. TENNESSEE
7. Oklahoma
8. CONNECTICUT
9. Rutgers
10. Baylor
11. Purdue
12. Georgia
13. Stanford
14. DePaul
15. Arizona State
16. Michigan State
17. Louisiana Tech
18. Utah
19. Temple
20. Texas A&M
21. UCLA
22. BYU
23. Bowling Green
24. New Mexico
25. Minnesota

2006-07

1. Duke
2. North Carolina
3. TENNESSEE
4. CONNECTICUT
5. Stanford
6. Maryland
7. Vanderbilt
8. Ohio State
9. Oklahoma
10. Arizona State
11. Purdue
12. LSU
13. Georgia
14. George Washington
15. Rutgers
16. Texas A&M
17. Middle Tenn. St.
18. N.C. State
19. Baylor
20. Bowling Green
21. Wisc. Green Bay
22. Marquette
23. Michigan State
24. Iowa State
25. Louisville

2007-2008

1. CONNECTICUT
2. North Carolina
3. TENNESSEE
4. Stanford
5. Maryland
6. LSU
7. Rutgers
8. Texas A&M
9. Duke
10. California
11. Old Dominion
12. Baylor
13. Oklahoma St
14. Oklahoma
15. Notre Dame
16. Kansas St.
17. West Virginia
18. Utah
19. Louisville
20. George Washington
21. Vanderbilt
22. Marist
23. UTEP
24. Virginia
25. Ohio St.

THE GREATEST TENNESSEE AND UCONN PLAYERS BY A VOTE OF OUR PEERS

1. Chamique Holdsclaw—Tennessee
2. Diana Taurasi—UConn
3. Candace Parker—Tennessee
4. Rebecca Lobo—UConn
5. Tamika Catchings—Tennessee
6. Sue Bird—UConn
7. Kara Wolters—UConn
8. Svetlana Abrosimova—Uconn
9. Maya Moore—UConn
10. Shea Ralph—UConn
11. Semeka Randall—Tennessee
12. Swin Cash—UConn
13. Jennifer Rizzotti—UConn
14. Nykesha Sales—UConn
15. Tamika Williams—UConn
16. Kara Lawson—Tennessee

17. Michelle Snow—Tennessee

18. Asjha Jones—UConn

19. Shrya Ely—UConn

20. Gwen Jackson—Tennessee

NCAA CHAMPIONS

YEAR	CHAMPION	SCORE	RUNNER-UP
1982	Louisiana Tech	76-62	Cheyney
1983	Southern California	69-67	Louisiana Tech
1984	Southern California	72-61	TENNESSEE
1985	Old Dominion	70-65	Georgia
1986	Texas	97-81	Southern California
1987	TENNESSEE	67-44	Louisiana Tech
1988	Louisiana Tech	56-54	Auburn
1989	TENNESSEE	76-60	Auburn
1990	Stanford	88-81	Auburn
1991	TENNESSEE	70-67	Virginia
1992	Stanford	78-62	Western Kentucky
1993	Texas Tech	84-82	Ohio State
1994	North Carolina	60-59	Louisiana Tech
1995	CONNECTICUT	70-64	TENNESSEE
1996	TENNESSEE	83-65	Georgia
1997	TENNESSEE	68-59	Old Dominion
1998	TENNESSEE	93-75	Louisiana Tech
1999	Purdue	62-45	Duke
2000	CONNECTICUT	72-51	TENNESSEE
2001	Notre Dame	68-66	Purdue
2002	CONNECTICUT	82-70	Oklahoma
2003	CONNECTICUT	73-68	TENNESSEE

YEAR	CHAMPION	SCORE	RUNNER-UP
2004	CONNECTICUT	70-61	TENNESSEE
2005	Baylor	84-62	Michigan State
2006	Maryland	78-75	Duke
2007	TENNESSEE	59-46	Rutgers
2008	TENNESSEE	64-48	Stanford

UCONN AND TENNESSEE PLAYERS WHO ARE CURRENTLY PLAYING IN THE WNBA

Asjah Jones, University of Connecticut 2002	Connecticut Sun
Nykesha Sales, University of Connecticut 1998	Connecticut Sun
Swin Cash, University of Connecticut 2001	Detroit Shock
Ann Strother, University of Connecticut 2006	Indiana Fever
Tamika Williams Raymond, University of Connecticut 2002	Minnesota Lynx
Diana Taurasi, University of Connecticut 2004	Phoenix Mercury
Sue Bird, University of Connecticut 2002	Seattle Storm
Barbara Turner, University of Connecticut 2006	Seattle Storm
Rita Williams, University of Connecticut 1998	Washington Mystics
Svetlana Abrosimova, University of Connecticut 2001	Minnesota Lynx
Tasha Butts, University of Tennessee 2004	Houston Comets
Tamika Catchings, University of Tennessee 2001	Indiana Fever
Chamique Holdsclaw, University of Tennessee 1999	Los Angeles Sparks
Sidney Spencer, University of Tennessee 2007	Los Angeles Sparks
Loree Moore, University of Tennessee 2005	New York Liberty
Kara Lawson, University of Tennessee 2003	Sacramento Monarchs
Shyra Ely, University of Tennessee 2005	Seattle Storm
Candace Parker, University of Tennessee 2008	Los Angeles Sparks
Ketia Swanier, University of Connecticut 2008	Connecticut Sun

Charde Houston, University of Connecticut 2008   Minnesota Lynx
Alexis Hornbuckle, University of Tennessee, 2008   Detroit Shock

ALL-TIME RESULTS

DATE	SCORE	PLACE
January 6, 2007	Tennessee 70 UConn 64	Hartford, Connecticut
January 7, 2006	Tennessee 89 UConn 80	Knoxville, Tennessee
January 8, 2005	Tennessee 68 UConn 67	Hartford, Connecticut
April 6, 2004	UConn 70 Tennessee 61	New Orleans, Louisiana
February 5, 2004	UConn 81 Tennessee 67	Knoxville, Tennessee
April 8, 2003	UConn 73 Tennessee 68	Atlanta, Georgia
January 4, 2003	UConn 63 Tennessee 62 (O.T.)	Hartford, Connecticut
March 29, 2002	UConn 79 Tennessee 56	San Antonio, Texas
January 5, 2002	UConn 86 Tennessee 72	Knoxville, Tennessee
February 2, 2001	Tennessee 92 UConn 88	Knoxville, Tennessee
December 30, 2000	UConn 81 Tennessee 76	Hartford, Connecticut
April 2, 2000	UConn 71 Tennessee 52	Philadelphia, Pennsylvania
February 2, 2000	Tennessee 72 UConn 71	Storrs, Connecticut

DATE	SCORE	PLACE
January 8, 2000	UConn 74 Tennessee 67	Knoxville, Tennessee
January 10, 1999	Tennessee 92 UConn 81	Hartford, Connecticut
January 3, 1998	Tennessee 84 UConn 69	Knoxville, Tennessee
March 24, 1997	Tennessee 91 UConn 81	Iowa City, Iowa
January 5, 1997	UConn 72 Tennessee 57	Hartford, Connecticut
March 29, 1996	Tennessee 88 UConn 83 (O.T.)	Charlotte, North Carolina
January 6, 1996	UConn 59 Tennessee 53	Knoxville, Tennessee
April 2, 1995	UConn 70 Tennessee 64	Minneapolis, Minnesota
January 16, 1995	UConn 77 Tennessee 66	Storrs, Connecticut

UCONN VS. TENNESSEE MATCHUPS ON T.V. RATINGS

UConn vs. Tennessee on ESPN

Year	Event	Rating
1995	Regular Season Jan. 16	1.0
1996	NCAA National Semifinal (Charlotte, N.C.)	2.5
1997	NCAA Regional Final (Iowa City, IA)	1.7
2000	Regular Season Feb. 2	1.0
2000	NCAA National Championship (Philadelphia)	3.5
2001	Regular Season Feb. 1	0.9
2002	NCAA National Semifinal (San Antonio)	2.5
2003	NCAA National Championship (Atlanta)	3.5
2004	Regular season Feb. 20	0.9

2004 NCAA National Championship (New Orleans) 4.3 HH—3,800,791 (ESPN's most-viewed and highest-rated college basketball game—men's or women's—in the network's history.)

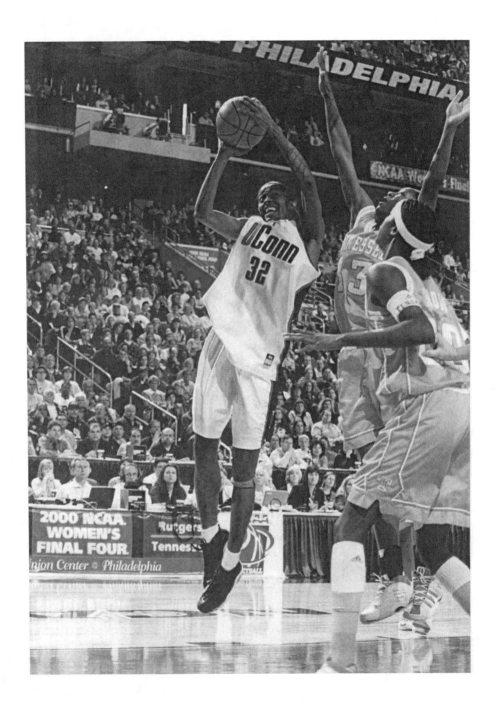

978-0-595-48737-0
0-595-48737-8

LaVergne, TN USA
12 December 2010
208443LV00002B/101/P